See the
Wider picture

Unbelievable umbrella street art

A colourful umbrella art installation floats above this promenade in
Águeda, Portugal. It casts a shadow of geometric shapes on the
ground below and fills the streets with a fairy tale-like atmosphere.
As well as providing shade in the heat of summer it also brings uplifting
energy and colour into a quiet street.

Is there anything similar in your country or town?

CONTENTS

Relationships; School; Present Simple; Wh- questions; Adverbs of frequency; Comparatives and superlatives

A new start at Belmont Academy

VOCABULARY
Relationships | School | Everyday technology | Holidays and travel | Means of transport | Opinion adjectives

GRAMMAR
Present Simple | Wh- questions | Adverbs of frequency | Comparatives and superlatives | Present Continuous | Past Simple | Present Perfect Simple with *for* and *since*

1 Write the correct word for each definition.

1 someone who studies with you in the same group **c** _l a s s m a t e_
2 a member of your family **r** _ _ _ _ _ _ _
3 your mother's mother **g** _ _ _ _
4 your father's (or mother's) brother **u** _ _ _ _
5 someone who lives near you **n** _ _ _ _ _ _ _ _

2 Complete the dialogue with the words below.

> always   do   doesn't   drives   ~~go~~   love   sometimes   studies   walk   where   who

Kay: Hi, I'm Kay. Do you ¹**go** to this school?

Jo: Yes, I ²_____. I'm a bit nervous because it's my first day here.

Kay: Oh, don't be nervous! I ³_____ studying here. Everyone is really friendly. My older sister ⁴_____ here too, but she ⁵_____ walk to school with me. Her boyfriend ⁶_____ her in his car.

Jo: ⁷_____ do you live? Is it near here?

Kay: Yes, it is. I usually ⁸_____ to school, but I ⁹_____ ride my bike when I don't have much time.

Jo: Oh, that's nice. And ¹⁰_____ do you hang out with here?

Kay: That's my group of friends over there. We ¹¹_____ arrive early so we can chat before class. Come on. I'll introduce you.

3 Choose the correct option.

1 (Physics) / Citizenship is my favourite subject at school. I like all the science subjects.
2 I've got exams at the end of the month, so I need to *revise / learn*.
3 At the end of the course there is a *practical / project* exam where you can show us what you know.
4 Our school has a new *canteen / computer lab* with twenty laptops.
5 I'm glad we don't have to wear a *uniform / prospectus* at our school. I like wearing my own clothes.
6 Our school has an interesting *curriculum / project*, with lots of different subjects to study.

4 Choose the correct option.

1 Our school is the *best / better / good* school in the area.
2 Sports lessons are *most / more / the most* interesting than Maths lessons.
3 Physics exams are the *worst / most / more* difficult.
4 The new computer lab is *bigger / biggest / big* than the old one.
5 It has *late / later / the latest* technology.
6 My new school is *the most exciting / exciting / more exciting* than my old school.

1 Choose the correct option.

1 (*Are you*) / *Do you* reading anything good at the moment?

No, *I'm not* / *I don't*. I'm too busy with homework.

2 What are you doing *exactly* / *right* now? Are you busy?

I not am doing / *I'm not doing* anything important. Do you need some help?

3 What are you *studying* / *study* in History class this year?

We *learn* / *'re learning* about the American civil war.

4 *Are* / *Do* you having a good time?

Yes, fantastic! *I'm talking* / *I'm always talking* to lots of very interesting people.

2 Complete the sentences with the Present Continuous form of the verbs below.

> call   enjoy   ~~have~~   not look forward to
> study   watch

1 Oh hi, Ben. **I'm having** lunch right now. Can I call you back?
2 What _____ (you) on TV? It looks interesting.
3 Ed _____ Maths class because he hasn't done his homework.
4 We _____ the Romans in History this month.
5 Where _____ (you) from? It sounds noisy.
6 _____ (you) your new school?

3 Use a word from each list to make phrases. Match the phrases with the pictures.

> chat   ~~make~~   text   upload   watch   write

> a blog   ~~a video~~   music videos   parents
> pictures   with friends

1   *make a video*   2 _____

3 _____   4 _____

5 _____   6 _____

4 Choose the correct option.

1 I'd like to (*write*) / *upload* a blog, but I just don't have enough time.
2 I prefer *texting* / *reading* e-books to traditional books because they're easier to carry around.
3 How often do you *watch* / *go online* to check your email?
4 For homework, we have to *write* / *film* a video of ourselves speaking English.
5 How can I *download* / *watch* songs to listen to on my phone?
6 When you take photos, do you *download* / *upload* them to a website or just keep them for yourself?

1 Mark the photos T (means of transport), H (type of holiday), A (accommodation) or Ac (activity). Then complete the words.

1 H b**e**a**c**h h**o**l**i**d**a**y   2 ☐ c _ _ _ _ _

3 ☐ h _ _ _ _ _ _   4 ☐ c _ _ _ _ _

5 ☐ c _ _ _ _ _ _ _ _   6 ☐ c _ _ _ _ _

2 Complete the crossword with the Past Simple form of the verbs.

		¹c
		a
		m
²	³	e
	⁴	
⁵		
⁶		
⁷		

Across
3 make   6 leave
4 go   7 have

Down
1 come   3 meet
2 spend   5 read

3 Complete the text with the Past Simple form of the verbs in brackets.

Last summer we ¹_went_ (go) on holiday to the south of France. We ²_____ (stay) on a campsite near the beach and we ³_____ (not do) much at all – just sunbathing. I ⁴_____ (read) a lot of books and it ⁵_____ (be) very relaxing. I also ⁶_____ (make) a lot of friends. In the evening we ⁷_____ (have) pizza together and then ⁸_____ (dance) at a local club. One night I ⁹_____ (not come) home until very late and my parents asked me, 'Where ¹⁰_____ (you/go)?' When I ¹¹_____ (tell) them, they ¹²_____ (not be) happy, but it was worth it! I hope we go there again next year.

4 Match 1–6 with a–f to make sentences.

1 b At what age can you drive
2 ☐ I would love to fly
3 ☐ Hurry up! We need to catch
4 ☐ My uncle taught me how to sail
5 ☐ Can we ride
6 ☐ Let's take

a the bus in ten minutes!
b a car in your country?
c a bus to London – it's cheaper than the train.
d a horse on the beach today?
e a helicopter one day.
f a yacht on holiday last year.

1 Look at the pictures. Order the letters and write the opinion adjectives.

1 nfuyn *funny*

2 alfwu _____

3 ngetciix _____

4 eussior _____

5 maweoes _____

6 isnoy _____

2 Write the correct opinion adjective for each definition.

1 something which you don't see every day
u_n_u_s_u_a_l

2 when something is the best it could be
p_ _ _ _ _ _t

3 something that is very bad t_ _ _ _ _ _ _e

4 very good a_ _ _ _ _g

5 not bad but not very good a_ _ _ _ _ _t

6 not interesting b_ _ _ _g

3 Complete the sentences with *for* or *since*.

1 I've known Hannah *since* we were three years old.

2 We've been at this school _____ six months.

3 Carla hasn't read a book _____ last February.

4 I've had my dog _____ nearly ten years.

5 They haven't watched a film at the cinema _____ ages.

6 I haven't eaten anything _____ breakfast.

4 Order the words to make sentences.

1 studied / have / abroad / ever / you / ?
Have you ever studied abroad?

2 yet / homework / Fiona / done / her / hasn't
_____

3 already / my parents / girlfriend / my / met / have
_____

4 the cat / has / fed / Mark / yet / ?
_____

5 camping / we / two / years / for / been / haven't
_____

6 just / the programme / started / has
_____

5 Complete the second sentence so that it means the same as the first one, using the words in brackets. Use no more than three words.

1 My family moved here in 2015. We live here now. (has)
My family *has lived here* since 2015.

2 I haven't been to China at any time in my life. (never)
I _____ to China.

3 We are still waiting for the class to start. (yet)
The class has _____.

4 There has never been a time in my life when I didn't like horror films. (always)
I _____ horror films.

5 Al met Sue six months ago. They are friends now. (for)
Al has known Sue _____.

6 Was there any time in your life when you had a pet cat? (ever)
Have _____ a pet cat?

1 Out of your comfort zone

1.1 **VOCABULARY** New experiences

I can talk about challenging new experiences and emotions.

1 ● Match the adjectives below with pictures 1–6. There are two extra adjectives.

| afraid annoyed ~~confused~~ joyful
| miserable relaxed stressed surprised

1 *confused*

2 _____

3 _____

4 _____

5 _____

6 _____

2 ●● How would you feel in each situation? Use the adjectives in Exercise 1.

1 You think you do well in an exam but then you get a bad mark.
  confused
2 You get a really good grade in an exam. _____
3 You're lying on the beach on holiday. _____
4 Your little brother breaks your phone. _____
5 You have lots of homework to do and don't have much time. _____
6 Your friend visits you and you weren't expecting it. _____
7 Your pet dies. _____
8 You're watching a horror film. _____

3 ●● Choose the adjective that does NOT fit in each sentence.

1 I feel ___ when I walk alone in the street at night.
 a uneasy (b) satisfied c anxious
2 Anna was ___ when she failed the exam.
 a relaxed b afraid c disappointed
3 The next time she took the exam, Anna was ___ to pass it.
 a determined b relaxed c satisfied
4 After spending weeks on their school project, Sue and Cameron were ___ when they finished.
 a joyful b satisfied c uneasy
5 People gave me lots of different advice about the exam, which made me feel ___.
 a stressed b joyful c confused
6 James was really ___ when he arrived at the station early and his train had already left.
 a miserable b annoyed c satisfied

4 ● **WORD FRIENDS** Choose the correct option.

1 (make) / get plans
2 boost / get a buzz out of something
3 boost / change your confidence
4 have / change your routine
5 give / have an adventure
6 give / get something a go
7 have / take something on board
8 say / give an opinion

5 ●● Complete what the people are saying with the words below.

afraid boosted change ~~determined~~
disappointed get have made stressed uneasy

1 This year has been so boring. I'm _determined_ to _____ an adventure this summer.

2 Some people _____ a buzz out of walking up mountains, but I'm _____ of heights!

3 Gillian _____ plans for the party weeks ago, so she'll be really _____ if we don't go.

4 Nick felt _____ when meeting new people, but then losing weight _____ his confidence.

5 I don't like it when I have to _____ my routine. It makes me feel _____.

6 ● Order the letters and complete the words in the sentences.

1 Sometimes it's difficult to **express** yourself clearly in a foreign language. (serpexs)
2 Why not **c**_____ yourself to try something new this week? (gellachen)
3 It's important to **k**_____ yourself and be realistic about what you can achieve. (wonk)
4 If you want to do more exercise, you should **m**_____ yourself wake up early and go to the gym. (keam)
5 Don't let miserable people damage your confidence. **B**_____ yourself and you'll be fine! (eb)
6 Try something difficult for a change. You might **s**_____ yourself and enjoy it! (purssier)

7 ●●● Complete the blog post with the words below.

anxious ~~challenged~~ congratulate
determined give make miserable
routine satisfied take

My thirty-day vegan challenge

This month I am getting out of my comfort zone! How? I've ¹challenged myself to stop eating any meat or animal products for thirty days. I'm not a vegetarian. In fact, I really like meat, but recently I read about the way many animals are treated and it made me feel really ² _____. I decided to ³ _____ this on board and ⁴ _____ a vegan diet a go.

I'm a bit ⁵ _____ about just eating vegetables and nuts all the time and I'm worried about getting hungry, but I'm ⁶ _____ to be successful, so I'm going to ⁷ _____ myself do this for the whole thirty days!

I've just finished my first day and I had lots of fruit for breakfast, and pasta with tomato sauce for lunch. I've changed my ⁸ _____ because I usually have only a small lunch. The good news is that I felt ⁹ _____ all afternoon and not hungry at all. In the evening I had a salad with nuts. A positive first day, I think, so time to ¹⁰ _____ myself!

Come back tomorrow to read about day 2!

I can use different tenses to talk about the present.

1 ● Match the verbs in bold in sentences 1–5 with functions a–e.

1 [c] I **know** the answer.
2 [ ] Chris **is doing** his homework.
3 [ ] Sara **works** in a hospital.
4 [ ] I'm **working** at a restaurant for the summer.
5 [ ] School **starts** at 8 a.m.

a a temporary situation
b a present action
c a state verb
d a routine
e a permanent situation

2 ● Complete the sentences with the Present Continuous form of the verbs below.

> discuss   leave   ~~not come~~   not have
> not live   rain   think

1 We don't need to wait for Gary – he *isn't coming* with us.
2 Oh no! It _____ ! We can't have a picnic now.
3 I _____ at home now. Builders are redecorating our house this month.
4 Cate _____ about starting dance classes.
5 Oh no! Jill and Charles _____ politics again!
6 _____ (you) already? You only got here a few minutes ago!
7 My brothers _____ dinner with us tonight. They're at a summer camp.

3 ●● Complete the sentences with the Present Simple or Present Continuous form of TWO of the verbs in brackets.

1 I *hear* you *'re learning* to play the drums – is that right? (hear / learn / think)
2 I usually _____ for the school bus, but this morning I _____ a lift from my dad. (get / take / wait)
3 Mia usually _____ to work, but today she _____ by train. (take / come / drive)
4 Quick, the film _____ ! You _____ the best part! (finish / miss / start)
5 I _____ my football coach because she always _____ me to do my best. (encourage / give / like)

4 ●● Find and correct the mistakes in the sentences. One sentence is correct.

1 My aunt and uncle ~~are having~~ two children. They're eight and twelve.
   have
2 I don't agree with the government's new education policy. What are you thinking?
   _____
3 Please don't disturb me. I'm doing my homework.
   _____
4 We stay in a different hotel this year because the place we usually stay in is closed for the summer.
   _____
5 Don't ask Phil for the answer. He isn't knowing.
   _____
6 Let's just sit down here. The game starts.
   _____

5 ●●● Complete the message with the Present Simple or Present Continuous form of the verbs below.

> close   do   enjoy   have (x2)   love   ~~not know~~
> not work   practise   sell   stay   want

Hey Ben!

How are things? I ¹*don't know* if you know, but I've got a summer job in Munich for a few weeks. I ²_____ with my German cousins who live here. It's great here and I ³_____ myself a lot.

I'm working in a small shop which ⁴_____ designer clothes and the other people here are really nice. We always ⁵_____ lots of fun in the day. In the evening when the shop ⁶_____ , we usually all ⁷_____ dinner together somewhere. I ⁸_____ Munich! It's a really interesting city and I ⁹_____ my German too!

What ¹⁰_____ (you) this summer? ¹¹_____ (you) to come and visit me in Munich? It would be great to see you again and there's lots of space at my cousins' house. I ¹²_____ at weekends, so we could spend some time together. Let me know!

Harry

I can identify specific detail in an article and talk about studying abroad.

1 Read the text. Match people A–F with the topics 1–6 they talk about.

1 ☐ crossing the street
2 ☐ how people behave
3 ☐ studying

4 ☐ making friends
5 ☐ losing something important
6 ☐ contacting your family

Challenging yourself abroad

Studying abroad is a big challenge for anyone to face and so it's natural to feel anxious when you're making plans. But that doesn't mean you shouldn't give it a go. We asked six international students to share their best advice for studying abroad.

A Maikel
From: Barcelona   **Studying in**: London
Try and learn something about the country before you go. Of course, you should learn the language and the basics — money, phones, etc., but it really helps if you can find out about the culture and the way people behave. You can find lots of information in books and on websites. Take it on board and you'll find it much easier to fit in.

B Tomasz
From: Kraków   **Studying in**: Paris
Scan copies of all your important documents before you leave — passport, visa, insurance documents, etc. I've lost my passport twice and both times it was a nightmare. I had to spend days at the embassy trying to get a new one and while you don't have it, you can't really do anything!

C Janice
From: London   **Studying in**: San Francisco
Learn the traffic rules! I got really stressed when I first came here because the cars drive on the other side of the road. I often got confused about where to look. Oh and 'jaywalking' (crossing the street in unauthorised places) is illegal here and you have to pay an expensive fine if a police officer sees you!

D Stephen
From: Birmingham   **Studying in**: Rio de Janeiro
You should definitely make friends with the locals because it will help you integrate. But I've learnt that it's also OK to make friends who are from your own country. It will help you feel less homesick and less miserable. Also, say 'yes' to every opportunity, even if you feel a bit uneasy at first. If you do, you'll have an adventure and see places you've never seen before. And may never see again!

E Özge
From: Istanbul   **Studying in**: Berlin
Keep a journal. Make yourself write something every day, even if it's just a sentence or two about what you've done that day. In a few years' time you'll get a buzz out of reading about your time abroad. And don't forget you're there to study. Meet new people and explore, but remember to go to class in the morning, even if it's not compulsory. Once you've studied, congratulate yourself, then go and have fun!

F Maria
From: Buenos Aires   **Studying in**: New York
Don't forget your family back home. As soon as you arrive, send them a message to say you've arrived safely and give them all your contact details. It's not difficult to stay in touch, but it's easy to forget in all the excitement of a new place. It will stop them feeling anxious about you and it will also make things easier for you, knowing the ones you love are easy to contact.

2 Read the text again. Mark the sentences T (true), F (false) or DS (doesn't say).

1 ☐ Maikel suggests using books and websites to learn the language before you go.
2 ☐ Tomasz didn't scan a copy of his passport.
3 ☐ It's against the law to cross the street anywhere you want in San Francisco.
4 ☐ Stephen thinks you should only spend time with local people.
5 ☐ Özge thinks you shouldn't go to classes if you don't have to.
6 ☐ Maria says it's easy to keep in contact with your family.

3 Find words or phrases in the text with the meanings below.

1 the most important and necessary facts about something   *the basics*
2 a very bad situation   _____
3 a punishment where you have to give money   _____
4 feel unhappy because you are a long way from home   _____
5 a book where you write things that happen to you each day   _____
6 you have to do it   _____
7 your phone number, home address, email address, etc.   _____

I can use different tenses to talk about past events and experiences.

1 ● Match questions 1–6 with answers a–f.

1 [c] What time did you get up this morning?

2 ☐ What were you doing at 10 p.m. last night?

3 ☐ Have you ever seen a lion in the wild?

4 ☐ What did you do on holiday?

5 ☐ Were you studying when the lights went out?

6 ☐ Have you done your English homework?

a No, I haven't. But I'd like to.

b Yes, I have. It took me hours!

c At 5.30 a.m.!

d Yes, I was.

e Very little. I mostly just sat on the beach.

f I was watching a film.

2 ● Choose the correct option. Then mark the sentences PS (Past Simple), PC (Past Continuous) or PP (Present Perfect).

1 Roshan *has had /* (*was having*) dinner with his family at 8 p.m. last night. **PC**

2 I *got up / was getting* early every day last week. _____

3 *Did you have / Have you ever* had an unusual pet? _____

4 When we left the cinema, it *rained / was raining*, so we got the bus home. _____

5 My older brother *became / has become* a father in 2014. _____

6 Jake isn't here. He *was going / 's gone* home already. _____

3 ●● Use the prompts to write sentences.

1 I / get / home / half an hour ago
   I got home half an hour ago.

2 my sister / start / school / last year

   _____

3 you / ever / play / baseball / ?

   _____

4 we / talk / about Susan / when / she walk / in

   _____

5 it / snow / when / I / wake up / this morning

   _____

6 when / I / be / little, / I / not like / broccoli

   _____

4 ●●● Complete the second sentence so that it means the same as the first one, using the word in brackets. Use between two and four words.

1 I went to New York at some point in my life. (been)
   I *have been to* New York.

2 Jay started watching a film at 7.30 p.m. and finished at 9 p.m. (was)
   Jay _____ at 8 p.m.

3 Fiona is not here now because she went to school earlier. (gone)
   Fiona _____ to school.

4 I started having a shower but didn't finish because the water went cold. (having)
   I _____ when the water went cold.

5 She didn't eat all morning and she didn't eat this afternoon. (hasn't)
   She _____ all day.

6 Paul went to Spain for the first time last year. He visited Madrid but he didn't go to Barcelona. (never)
   Paul _____ to Barcelona.

5 ●●● Complete the dialogue with the correct form of the verbs below.

> b̶e̶ come climb do fall stay
> visit walk

A: Hey, Nikki. How ¹*was* your holiday?

B: Great, thanks! I ² _____ a really big mountain!

A: Wow! Really?

B: Yes, it was amazing – the most exciting thing I ³ _____ ever _____, actually!

A: Really? Where did you go?

B: Well, while I ⁴ _____ with my cousin in Scotland, we decided to climb Ben Nevis. It's the highest mountain in Britain.

A: How was it?

B: Amazing, but while we ⁵ _____ up, one of the people with us ⁶ _____ and broke her leg.

A: Oh no! What happened?

B: Well, a helicopter ⁷ _____ and took her to hospital. She's better now, thank goodness. What about you? How was your holiday?

A: Not as exciting as yours – I just ⁸ _____ my gran in the country.

I can identify specific detail in a radio programme and talk about personality.

1 Complete the crossword with adjectives of personality.

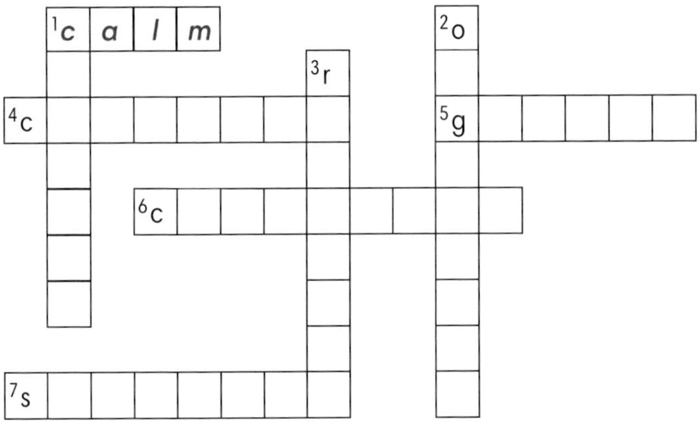

¹c	a	l	m			²o	

(crossword grid)
- 1 Across: calm
- 3 Down: r
- 4 Across: c
- 5 Across: g
- 6 Across: c
- 7 Across: s

Across

1 If you can keep *calm* in a stressful situation, then you'll be fine.

4 I'd love to do a job where I can be _____, thinking of new ideas every day.

5 My grandfather was a very _____, caring man. He wouldn't hurt a fly!

6 If you're going to succeed in life, you need to be _____ and believe you can do anything.

7 My sister is the _____ one in our family. She always makes the right decisions.

Down

1 Will's a very _____ boy – he's always asking questions about everything.

2 I wish I was more _____. My things are always in a mess and I can never find anything!

3 You can trust Sandy. She's very _____.

2 🔊 02 Listen to an interview with Miles Baker, a projection mapper. Put the topics a–d in the order he talks about them.

a ☐ the different uses of projection mapping

b ☐ the history of projection mapping

c ☐ why he enjoys his work

d ☐ an explanation of what projection mapping is

3 🔊 02 Listen again. Complete the notes with the missing information.

All about projection mapping

- Projecting an ¹*image* onto something, e.g. the ² _____ of a building or ³ _____ a theatre.

- Often includes sound and together they tell a ⁴ _____.

- First started in the ⁵ _____. One of the first displays was in Disneyland.

- Uses: art, advertising, ⁶ _____, restaurants, appliances in modern homes, e.g. ⁷ _____.

I can ask for and offer help, and respond to offers of help.

1 Order the words to make questions.

1 me / a hand / something / can / give / you / with / ?
Can you give me a hand with something?

2 else / need / you / do / anything / ?
_____

3 you / get / can / anything / I / ?
_____

4 you / excuse me, / me / would / helping / mind / ?
_____

5 me / could / help / you / ?
_____

6 a hand / can / you / give / I / ?
_____

7 help / may / you / I / ?
_____

2 Write the questions from Exercise 1 in the correct column.

Asking for help
Can you give me a hand with something?
Offering help

3 Match questions 1–7 with responses a–g.

1 [b] Can I get you anything to drink?
2 [ ] This exercise is too difficult. Can you help me?
3 [ ] May I help you? You look lost.
4 [ ] You seem stressed. Can I give you a hand?
5 [ ] Can you give me a hand with these bags?
6 [ ] Excuse me, would you mind helping me? I'm looking for the staff room.
7 [ ] Here are the books you ordered. Do you need anything else?

a That would be great, thanks. I just don't understand this Maths problem.
b No, thanks. I'm fine.
c That's really nice of you, thanks. I'm looking for the station.
d No, these are all I need. Thanks for your help.
e No, of course not! I'll show you.
f Sure! I'll be with you in a minute.
g Of course! Let me carry these two for you.

4 🔊 03 Complete the dialogue with one word in each gap. Listen and check.

Jesse: Hi, Steph. Sorry to disturb you, but could you give me a ¹*hand* with something?

Steph: ²_____! I'll be with you in a ³_____. … Sorry about that. What can I help you with?

Jesse: I'm having problems with my Maths homework – it's really difficult. Would you ⁴_____ helping me?

Steph: Oh sorry, Jesse. I'm really bad at Maths!

Matt: Can I ⁵_____ you a hand, Jesse? Maths is my best subject.

Jesse: That's really ⁶_____ of you, Matt, thanks. Could you ⁷_____ me with number three, here?

Matt: Of course! Let me look. Oh, it's simple – see? You just need to add these two numbers together and divide the total by this number.

Jesse: Ah, I see! Thanks for ⁸_____!

Matt: No problem. Do you need anything ⁹_____?

Jesse: No, I'm ¹⁰_____, thanks.

5 Match sentences 1–2 with responses a–b.

OUT of class

1 [ ] Catch you later!
2 [ ] You made me jump!

a Sorry! I didn't mean to scare you.
b Bye!

I can write a description of a personal challenge.

1 **Match the verbs below with the definitions.**

~~gasp~~ scream shake shiver sweat yawn

1 breathe in suddenly and loudly because you're surprised or in pain _gasp_
2 produce liquid on the surface of your skin because you're hot or nervous _____
3 when part, or all, of your body moves quickly because you're afraid or cold _____ / _____
4 make a loud, high noise because you're afraid or hurt _____
5 open your mouth wide and breathe in because you're tired or bored _____

2 **Complete Antje's description of a personal challenge with phrases a–f.**

a One day I heard about a school talent show
b I've always loved
c The experience boosted
d When I arrived at
e The problem is,
f At the beginning, it was difficult

My first performance
by Antje Fischer

¹*I've always loved* singing and I sing whenever I can at home – usually in the shower! ²_____ I've always hated the thought of singing in public or even in front of my closest friends. The thought of it makes me feel really anxious. ³_____, however, and I decided to give it a go.

⁴_____ the contest, I walked onto the stage and I was terrified. My hands were shaking and I could hardly hold the microphone. When the music started, I was shivering all over, but I began to sing the first few words. ⁵_____, but gradually I started to calm down and sing normally. I actually loved it and by the end, I wanted to scream with joy!

I didn't win the contest but people said I sang well. ⁶_____ my confidence about my singing and now I'm thinking about joining a band.

3 **Match 1–6 with a–f to make sentences.**

1 [d] I first realised I had a problem
2 [ ] Soon after that
3 [ ] So I decided to give
4 [ ] Suddenly, somebody
5 [ ] That day I learnt
6 [ ] Now I'm not afraid

a of heights any more.
b screamed!
c something important about myself.
d when I went climbing with a friend.
e I heard someone shout, 'Come on, Dan!'
f it a go.

4 **Complete Toby's notes about a personal challenge he did with phrases a–e.**

a he told me to look at the distance, not the water
b always been afraid of water
c feel more confident on the water now
d realised when I travelled by ferry as a child
e nervous at first, shivering and sweating

Sailing a boat
Background
• ¹_always been afraid of water_
  ²_____

• uncle has a boat, invited us to go sailing
What happened
• ³_____

• suddenly, my uncle gave me the controls
  ⁴_____

• slowly felt more confident
How I felt after the challenge
• loved it
• want to do it again
• ⁵_____

5 **Look at the notes in Exercise 4. Write a description of Toby's personal challenge. Follow the instructions below.**

1 Use the text in Exercise 2 as a model.
2 Write three paragraphs:
   • the background to the challenge
   • a description of what happened
   • how Toby felt after the challenge.
3 Use vocabulary from Exercise 1.
4 Use phrases from Exercises 2 and 3.

For each learning objective, tick (✓) the box that best matches your ability.

☺☺ = I understand and can help a friend.   ☹ = I understand but have some questions.

☺ = I understand and can do it by myself.   ☹☹ = I do not understand.

		☺☺	☺	☹	☹☹	Need help?	Now try ...
1.1	Vocabulary					Students' Book pp. 10–11 Workbook pp. 6–7	Ex. 1–2, p. 15
1.2	Grammar					Students' Book p. 12 Workbook p. 8	Ex. 3–4, p. 15
1.3	Reading					Students' Book p. 13 Workbook p. 9	
1.4	Grammar					Students' Book p. 14 Workbook p. 10	Ex. 4–5, p. 15
1.5	Listening					Students' Book p. 15 Workbook p. 11	
1.6	Speaking					Students' Book p. 16 Workbook p. 12	Ex. 6, p. 15
1.7	Writing					Students' Book p. 17 Workbook p. 13	

1.1   I can talk about challenging new experiences and emotions.
1.2   I can use different tenses to talk about the present.
1.3   I can identify specific detail in an article and talk about studying abroad.
1.4   I can use different tenses to talk about past events and experiences.
1.5   I can identify specific detail in a radio programme and talk about personality.
1.6   I can ask for and offer help, and respond to offers of help.
1.7   I can write a description of a personal challenge.

What can you remember from this unit?

New words I learned (the words you most want to remember from this unit)	**Expressions and phrases I liked** (any expressions or phrases you think sound nice, useful or funny)	**English I heard or read outside class** (e.g. from websites, books, adverts, films, music)

Vocabulary

1 Choose the correct option.

1 I was *surprised / anxious* to see Carla at school today. I thought she was ill.

2 I felt *joyful / uneasy* walking down that street the other night because it was very dark.

3 I hope you *take / have* this advice on board and work harder in the future.

4 Our teacher likes us to be *punctual / fussy* for class. She hates it when we're late.

5 James is so *gentle / generous*. He always gives people big presents on their birthday.

6 When you succeed at a new challenge, it can *boost / change* your confidence.

2 Complete the sentences with the verbs below.

| be congratulate express know surprise tell |

1 Don't try and be something you're not. Just _____ yourself and relax.

2 If you work hard and study, you might _____ yourself and pass the exam!

3 Be confident. If you _____ yourself that you can do it, then you'll succeed.

4 At first, it's often difficult to _____ yourself in another language.

5 Don't push too hard. _____ yourself, your limits and when it's time to stop.

6 I think you should always _____ yourself if you've done something well or succeeded in a personal challenge.

Grammar

3 Complete the sentences with the Present Simple or Present Continuous form of the verbs in brackets.

1 We _____ (stay) in a hotel at the moment, until we can move into our new house.

2 Jake _____ (get up) at 6 a.m. every morning, except on Sundays.

3 My cousin _____ (be) a marine biologist.

4 Can I call you back? I _____ (have) lunch at the moment.

5 Sally _____ (not enjoy) this film and wants to leave the cinema.

6 _____ (your mum/like) her new job?

4 Choose the correct option.

1 We *had / were having* a picnic when it started to rain.

2 I *didn't pass / wasn't passing* my driving test last week.

3 Chris *never climbed / has never climbed* a mountain.

4 Susie *wasn't / hasn't been* here last week because she was on holiday.

5 We *went / were going* to a new school last year.

6 I *was watching / have watched* a film when you phoned me.

5 Complete the text with the Past Simple, Past Continuous or Present Perfect form of the verbs in brackets.

I ^{1}_____ (always/love) travelling to new places, so last summer I ^{2}_____ (decide) to travel around Italy by train with some friends and Clara, my cousin. It ^{3}_____ (be) a great experience. We ^{4}_____ (see) lots of great places and ^{5}_____ (talk) to lots of interesting people, but it wasn't all good. While we ^{6}_____ (walk) around Rome, someone stole Clara's bag with all her money and passport! We spent the next day at the embassy getting a new one. While we ^{7}_____ (wait) at the embassy, we ^{8}_____ (meet) a friend of Clara's from university and she ^{9}_____ (invite) us to stay with her for the rest of the week!

Speaking language practice

6 Complete the dialogues with one word in each gap.

1 A: Excuse me, would you _____ helping me?
   B: No, of course _____ .

2 A: Can I _____ you anything?
   B: No, I'm _____ , but thanks anyway.

3 A: Can I give you a _____ ?
   B: That's really _____ of you, thanks.

4 A: Could you _____ me with this?
   B: Sure! I'll be with you in a _____ .

5 A: Can you _____ me a hand with something?
   B: Of course! What _____ I do for you?

1 Match 1–5 with a–e to make phrases from the text.

1 [e] sand   a peaks
2 [ ] world   b test
3 [ ] highest   c terrain
4 [ ] endurance   d championship
5 [ ] difficult   e dunes

2 Complete the sentences with the phrases from Exercise 1.

1 *Sand dunes* in the desert change constantly because of the wind.
2 Most climbers would love to climb all the world's _____.
3 I'm doing the London marathon next year – it's going to be a real _____ for me!
4 Most sports have a(n) _____ once a year in which the best competitors participate.
5 The athletes had to run through very _____, including deserts and mountains.

3 Choose the correct option.

1 Running the marathon was really *traditional* / (*tough*), but I'm glad I did it!
2 The most *challenging* / *stressed* race I've ever taken part in was a half marathon.
3 The Ironman bike ride is a *long-distance* / *one-day* race of 180 km.
4 Michael is very *competitive* / *popular* – he hates losing!
5 Before the race I felt really *tough* / *stressed*, but I relaxed after I started running.

4 Complete the sentences with the verbs below. There is one extra verb.

> complete   cross   ~~hold~~   last   push
> suffer   take part

1 We are going to *hold* our school sports day on the last day of term.
2 Would you like to _____ in a marathon?
3 Athletes really have to _____ themselves in order to complete the race.
4 Sarah wants to _____ the swim in three hours.
5 Athletes have to _____ part of the Sahara desert during this long-distance race!
6 The race will _____ for three days in total.

5 Look at the photos and add the missing vowels to complete the phrases.

1 v _ _ l _ nt sandstorms
2 h _ st _ l _ desert

3 _ npr _ d _ ct _ bl _ camels
4 _ xtr _ m _ heat

6 Use the prompts to write sentences. Use the tense in brackets.

1 they / enter / the largest sand desert in the world (Present Continuous)
 They are entering the largest sand desert in the world.
2 they / already / cross / the Atlantic Ocean (Present Perfect)
 _____
3 unfortunately, / they / get / lost (Past Simple)
 _____
4 they / complete / an almost impossible journey (Present Perfect)
 _____
5 they / still / be / friends / at the end of it (Present Simple)
 _____

7 Complete the sentences with the nouns below.

> ~~dehydration~~   destination   expedition
> explorer   temperature   well

1 Jane didn't drink enough water and was suffering from *dehydration*.
2 They are going on a(n) _____ into the jungles of South America.
3 The travellers drank water from the _____.
4 Wilfrid Thesiger was a famous British _____.
5 The _____ reached 47°C.
6 James and Ben's final _____ was a place called Umm as Sammim.

8 Read the video script. Underline any words or phrases you don't know and find their meaning in your dictionary.

Part 1: The adventure begins

Olympian James Cracknell and adventurer Ben Fogel are entering the largest sand desert in the world – The Empty Quarter in the Middle East – for their next big challenge. They

5 are travelling in the footsteps of legendary British explorer Wilfred Thesiger. Their goal? To recover their lost friendship. Now, in the most hostile desert on the planet, they will face extreme heat and dehydration … violent sandstorms … and unpredictable camels.

10 And they will have terrible arguments.
Can James and Ben find what they are looking for in the most remote place on earth? They have been on lots of expeditions but this one is the hardest of all.

Part 2: An almost impossible journey

15 This is James and Ben's third expedition in the last decade. They have already crossed the Atlantic Ocean and raced to the South Pole. This is the Empty Quarter.
They start the journey in Mandar and travel through the country of Oman close to the border with Saudi Arabia. Their

20 destination? The quicksands at Umm as Sammim, which Thesiger saw in the 1940s. They have eight days to travel the 250 kilometres. In those eight days they have to survive on dried camel meat, dates and flat bread. And plenty of water – temperatures can reach 47°C out in the desert at this time of

25 year. They need to drink ten litres per day and water wells are not easy to find. Luckily, their trusted camels can carry it all. They find the way only with a map and compasses. Unfortunately, they got lost. They took eleven days to make the trip but finally they arrived at the quicksands. It's not an oasis –

30 there are no trees or even water here but it was their goal, their challenge. They are so relieved to be here at last. In the end, they hug each other … and the camels who helped them. They have completed an almost impossible journey – to one of the most remote places on earth and they are still friends at

35 the end of it!

2

What a waste!

VOCABULARY
Pollution | Protecting and damaging the environment | Compound nouns: the environment | Elections and campaigns

GRAMMAR
Past Perfect | *used to*

READING
Multiple choice

LISTENING
Listening for specific detail

SPEAKING
Agreeing and disagreeing

ENGLISH IN USE
Question tags

BBC CULTURE
When will the lights go out?

I can talk about pollution and the environment.

1 ● Find nine environment words in the wordsearch.

S	L	I	T	T	E	R	R	R	P
S	A	P	R	E	P	L	A	N	T
R	I	E	A	D	W	J	K	T	H
U	F	T	F	A	C	T	O	R	Y
B	I	R	F	F	A	C	T	G	S
B	N	O	I	H	T	C	O	I	L
I	G	L	C	R	Z	H	H	J	E
S	N	R	H	R	S	M	O	K	E
H	E	E	H	A	H	D	H	T	V
E	N	D	A	N	G	E	R	E	D

1 l i t t e r
2 p _ _ _ _ _ l
3 t _ _ _ _ _ _ c
4 r _ _ _ _ _ _ h
5 f _ _ _ _ _ _ y
6 o _ _
7 s _ _ _ _ e
8 e _ _ _ _ _ _ _ _ _ _ d animal
9 p _ _ _ t

2 ●● Choose the correct option.

1 Ugh, this cheese is old. I'll throw it in the *litter* / *bin*
2 After they built the new road, there was less *petrol* / *traffic* in the city centre.
3 The company closed the *factory* / *bin* after complaints about pollution from local residents.
4 It's becoming more and more difficult to find new sources of *smoke* / *oil* in the world.
5 Does your car run on *oil* / *petrol* or gas?
6 The forest fire was in an area with lots of *endangered* / *rubbish* animals.

3 ● **WORD FRIENDS** Match verbs 1–4 with their opposites a–d.

1 [d] recycle
2 [ ] protect
3 [ ] pollute
4 [ ] save

a clean up
b waste
c damage
d throw away

4 ● **WORD FRIENDS** Match 1–7 with a–g to make sentences.

1 [b] We're going to be late – our bus is stuck in a traffic
2 [ ] You separate your glass bottles at the bottle
3 [ ] We need to use more types of renewable
4 [ ] It's incredible that some people don't believe that climate
5 [ ] We take our bottles and cans to a recycling
6 [ ] I use public
7 [ ] We should stop at this petrol

a change is real.
b jam.
c station. There isn't another one for 200 miles.
d transport when I can because it's better for the environment.
e bank into different colours of glass.
f energy, such as wind and solar power.
g centre next to the supermarket.

5 ●● Complete the comments with the words below.

> bank ~~bin~~ change endangered factories litter oil recycling traffic transport

1   Too many people throw away bottles in the *bin*. They should take them to a bottle _____ .

2   Using _____ as an energy source is one of the biggest causes of climate _____ .

3   Since the government improved public _____ in this city, there are fewer _____ jams in the morning.

4   Our city needs more _____ centres. I often see people throw away bottles and cans as _____ .

5   Water and land pollution from the _____ in the area affects _____ animals.

6 ●● Choose the word or phrase that does NOT fit in each sentence.

1   Do you ___ plastic bags at home?
    a   recycle   (b)   pollute
    c   throw away

2   What do people in your country do to ___ the environment?
    a   recycle   b   protect   c   damage

3   The main aim of our green group is to protect the ___ .
    a   environment   b   ocean   c   rubbish

4   Personally, I don't do much to ___ beaches.
    a   pollute   b   clean up   c   waste

5   My school ___ a lot of energy every month.
    a   throws away   b   saves   c   wastes

6   Every year there are more and more endangered ___ in the world.
    a   plants   b   stations   c   animals

7   We should do everything we can to save ___ .
    a   water   b   pollution   c   energy

7 ●● Find and correct the wrong words in the sentences.

1   Let's take these newspapers and magazines to the recycling ~~bank~~.   *centre*

2   The local government has decided to clean out the local beaches.   _____

3   Throwing away plastic bags and other litter protects the environment.   _____

4   I listened to a talk last night about climate energy – it's a huge problem.   _____

5   The litter from these factories has caused a lot of air pollution.   _____

6   Over 1,000 plants and animals in the USA are renewable. They may not exist in a few years.
    _____

8 ●●● Complete the blog post with one word in each gap.

The time for change is now

It's difficult to understand why people don't want to ¹*protect* the planet more. It's a really big problem and we are already seeing the effects of climate ²_____ . People still drive their cars everywhere and refuse to use ³_____ transport. Traffic ⁴_____ which ⁵_____ the air are common in big cities. And we ⁶_____ away plastic bags and aluminium cans, which we should ⁷_____ . We need to move to 100 percent ⁸_____ energy and stop depending on petrol and ⁹_____ . We need to ¹⁰_____ up the oceans and the air. And we need to do it now or our children may not have a planet to live on.

I can talk about past events using the Past Perfect.

1 ● **Complete the sentences with the Past Perfect form of the verbs in brackets.**

1 By the time she was twenty, Silvia _had travelled_ (travel) all over the world.

2 They were hungry because they _____ (not eat) their breakfast.

3 _____ (you/finish) your homework before you went out last night?

4 Five minutes into the film, I realised I _____ (see) it before.

5 _____ (you/try) Mexican food before you went to that restaurant?

6 James was satisfied when he changed class because he _____ (not be) happy there for a long time.

2 ● **Choose the correct option.**

1 We were very tired because we *went* / (*had gone*) to bed late the night before.

2 Had you ever visited a zoo before you *went* / *had been* there last month?

3 We *waited* / *had waited* in line for two hours when the ticket office finally opened.

4 I *had already read* / *already read* the book, so I knew how the film ended.

5 When Katie finally *passed* / *had passed* her piano exam, she had taken it five times!

6 When I got to class, I realised I *forgot* / *had forgotten* to bring my homework.

7 We *arrived* / *had arrived* late at the zoo and it had already closed.

8 My parents had already left for work when I *got up* / *had got up* this morning.

3 ●● **Use the prompts to write sentences.**

1 Angela / not study / English / before / she / visit / London
Angela hadn't studied English before she visited London.

2 by / time / I / finish / school yesterday / it / get / dark outside
_____

3 how long / you / have / your bike / when / somebody / steal / it / ?
_____

4 when / we / arrived / at the cinema / the film / already / start
_____

5 I / just / arrived / at the party / when / it / finish
_____

6 Kayla / be / tired / because / she / not sleep / well
_____

7 Chiara / never / see / a volcano / before / she / go / to Indonesia
_____

8 by / time / I / get up / my brother / eat / all the pancakes
_____

4 ●●● **Read the text. Choose the correct answers.**

People [1]_____ much when my parents were my age. Until a big recycling centre [2]_____ in their town, people [3]_____ things before. They [4]_____ thrown away aluminium cans, bottles and plastic bags. There wasn't as much packaging and so it [5]_____ a big problem like it is today. The first time they [6]_____ to the recycling centre, they [7]_____ all the rubbish from home with them! They [8]_____ that not everything is recyclable! Nowadays it's much easier – there is a collection service which takes things from your house. But you still have to remember to put the bin out early. Yesterday I [9]_____ and by the time I put it out, the truck [10]_____.

1 **a** didn't recycle   **b** hadn't recycled   **c** recycled
2 **a** had opened   **b** didn't open   **c** opened
3 **a** didn't recycle   **b** recycled   **c** hadn't recycled
4 **a** had   **b** were   **c** used
5 **a** didn't   **b** wasn't   **c** hadn't
6 **a** had been   **b** didn't go   **c** went
7 **a** takes   **b** hadn't taken   **c** took
8 **a** realised   **b** hadn't realised   **c** had realised
9 **a** had forgotten   **b** forgot   **c** hadn't forgotten
10 **a** had already left **b** already left   **c** left

I can understand the main points and identify specific detail in an article.

1 Match the phrases below with definitions 1–5.

> environmental laws   ~~greenhouse gases~~   sign a petition
> take legal action   win a court case

1 carbon dioxide and methane are examples of these *greenhouse gases*

2 add your name to a list of people who are asking the government to do something _____

3 successfully challenge a person or organisation in court _____

4 rules that people and businesses must follow which protect the land, sea and air _____

5 try to change a situation using lawyers _____

2 Read the article. Match headings a–e with paragraphs 1–4. There is one extra heading.

a Other ways the organisation helps

b Victory for four green teens

c Future plans

d Why was the victory so important?

e The organisation that supported them

3 Read the article again. Choose the correct answers.

1 The Global Warming Solutions Act
 a tried to stop all greenhouse gases immediately.
 b was rejected by the government in the 1990s.
 c tried to reduce greenhouse gases all over the USA.
 d made a lot of people angry.

2 Why was this an important win?
 a It was the first victory against the state government since 2008.
 b Because it means the state must now clean up the air.
 c Because it means the state must now reduce energy costs.
 d Because it was the first court case about the environment.

3 Our Children's Trust
 a is a government organisation.
 b trains young people to become lawyers when they're older.
 c educates and supports young people who want to take legal action.
 d thinks not many young people care about the environment.

4 What do the people at Our Children's Trust believe?
 a We can't wait any longer to save the environment.
 b Children cause environmental problems.
 c No governments are taking any action.
 d The Global Warming Solutions Act isn't good enough.

Teenagers against climate change

1 _____

Four teenagers in the USA have recently won an important court case against the Massachusetts state government to make them reduce greenhouse gases. The 2008 Global Warming Solutions Act says that all state governments must reduce greenhouse gases by 20 percent. In 2012, the Massachusetts state government hadn't done anything and so hundreds of young people signed a petition. The Massachusetts state government still didn't do anything, so the teenagers took the state government to court. The teenagers lost their first court case, but last week another judge decided that the state government was wrong and it must now improve traffic and use more renewable energy.

2 _____

The teenagers were working with Our Children's Trust, an organisation which uses legal action when local governments don't follow environmental laws. The organisation was started in Oregon in 2011 and they encourage and train young people to get involved in environmental change. Our Children's Trust knew that the biggest supporters of action against climate change are usually young people and so they wanted to help make their voices heard by governments who were not doing enough.

3 _____

The organisation believes that we must act against climate change urgently, so that the children of the future can have a clean and safe world to live in. They are involved in lots of similar cases with other state governments at the moment. They also make short films to educate people about the environmental problems we face in the world today.

4 _____

The victory in Massachusetts was a huge success, not only for the state, but for young people in general, as it has shown that young people really do have a voice. Governments cannot sit and do nothing anymore when people are polluting the air.

I can talk about repeated past actions that no longer happen.

1 ● Match 1–5 with a–e to make sentences.

1 [d] I didn't use to like many vegetables,
2 [ ] We used to throw away all our rubbish,
3 [ ] We used to use a lot of oil for fuel in my country,
4 [ ] Sara didn't use to work hard at school,
5 [ ] Paula used to throw away litter,

a but now she studies all the time.
b but now we use more renewable energy.
c but now she always puts it in the bin.
d but now I like most of them.
e but these days we recycle nearly everything.

2 ● Order the words to make sentences.

1 used to / water / waste / we / a lot of
   We used to waste a lot of water.

2 recycle / plastic bags / Jamie / use to / didn't
   _____

3 I / use to / worry / didn't / about / climate change
   _____

4 use / to / where / live / you / did / ?
   _____

5 throw / used to / my mum / away / paper
   _____

6 did / sing / use to / in a band / Ella / ?
   _____

3 ●● Complete the sentences with the correct form of *used to* and the verbs below.

| be   live   not have   not watch   ~~play~~   travel

1 My dad _used to play_ football for a club when he was younger, but now he doesn't do any sport at all.
2 Where _____ (you) before you moved to this street?
3 My grandparents _____ TV when they were children.
4 We _____ a recycling centre in our town, so it was difficult to recycle anything.
5 We _____ everywhere by car, but now we use public transport more.
6 _____ (there) a lot of smoke in the air here before they closed the factory?

4 ●● Complete the second sentence so it has the same meaning as the first one. Use the correct form of *used to.*

1 When I was little, I played with toys every day.
   I _used to play_ with toys every day.
2 My grandparents' generation didn't recycle rubbish.
   My grandparents' generation _____ rubbish.
3 Did you play video games every day when you were younger?
   Did you _____ every day when you were younger?
4 When he was my age, my dad worked in a shop at the weekend.
   When he was my age, my dad _____ in a shop at the weekend.
5 My uncle lived on a boat when he was my age.
   My uncle _____ in a house when he was my age.

5 ●●● Find and correct five mistakes in the text.

Recycling through the ages

Many people think that recycling is a new thing, but in fact, humans used to recycle things in 400 B.C.! Scientists recently ~~used to discover~~ that people in Turkey reused glass. Later, in 1031, the Japanese used to start recycling paper.

In times when people were poor, they didn't used to throw things away. Just before the industrial revolution (1760–1830), people use to melt and recycle metals. But during the industrial revolution, things suddenly became cheaper and easier to make, so there was less recycling.

Nowadays we recycle because we know more about environmental problems. So while your grandparents used to recycled because they had to, we now recycle because we should.

1 _discovered_   4 _____
2 _____   5 _____
3 _____

6 Choose the correct option.

1 A: *Ouch!* / *Take care!*
   B: Are you OK?
2 A: Look at this place! There's rubbish everywhere.
   B: I know. *It's a shame, really.* / *Take care.*

OUT of **class**

I can identify specific details in short dialogues.

1 Complete the words in the sentences.

1 Every year we have the chance to **v** _o_ _t_ _e_ for a new class president.

2 Our group has decided we'd like to **o** _ _ _ _ _ _ _ an event at school to raise money for environmental projects.

3 The government has decided to **h** _ _ _ an election this May.

4 Jackie wants to **s** _ _ _ _ **u** _ to help clean the river bank at the weekend.

5 After seeing the pollution of the ocean on holiday, I decided to **j** _ _ _ a campaign to raise awareness of the problem.

6 My dad advised me to **b** _ _ _ _ _ a member of an environmental group if I want to do something to help the environment.

2 🔊 04 **Listen to four dialogues. Choose the correct answers.**

1 What did Tara do in the holidays?

2 What has Tyler James done?

3 What activity will Kerry's group do next?

4 What does Paul think we need more of?

3 🔊 04 **Listen again. Mark the sentences T (true) or F (false).**

1 ☐ Tara's friend didn't know what a green camp was.

2 ☐ At green camp they learned about protecting animals and the environment.

3 ☐ Tyler James has always been very 'green'.

4 ☐ Kerry's dad thinks she did a good thing at school today.

5 ☐ Paul thinks public transport makes the air dirty.

I can agree and disagree with other people's point of view.

1 Match 1–6 with a–f to make phrases.

1	[c] Maybe	a	sure about that.
2	[ ] I totally	b	don't agree.
3	[ ] That's not	c	you're right.
4	[ ] I'm not	d	agree.
5	[ ] I think that's a	e	great idea.
6	[ ] Really? I	f	always true.

2 Order the words to make phrases.

1 think / too / I / so
I think so too.

2 should … / I / we / think / don't
_____

3 disagree / I / totally
_____

4 that / say / again / can / you / !
_____

5 so / suppose / I
_____

3 Write the phrases from Exercises 1 and 2 in the correct column.

Agreeing	Disagreeing
Maybe you're right.	_____
_____	_____
_____	_____
_____	_____
_____	

4 Complete the dialogues with phrases a–c.

OUT of class

a Try it out!
b Let's get started!
c You can say that again!

1 A: That looks heavy.
   B: _____ Would you mind helping me carry it?

2 A: We don't have much time left.

   B: Alright, alright! Give me a chance to get ready, then we can begin.

3 A: Go on. _____ You might like it!
   B: OK. Wow! It's great! You were right!

5 🔊 05 Complete the dialogue with one word in each gap. Listen and check.

Kayla: OK. Let's ¹*get* started. So what ideas do we have for the class environmental project?

Dan: Well, I thought we could organise a garage sale to raise money for an environmental organisation.

Kayla: I'm not ²_____ about that. I think the idea is to do something that the whole class can get involved in, rather than just raise money for a charity.

Dan: Yeah, maybe you're ³_____.

Anne: I ⁴_____ so too. I thought we could give a presentation on different ways to save energy at home.

Dan: I don't think we ⁵_____ limit ourselves like that. What about something where we take direct action? Could we go and collect plastic bags and aluminium cans, then recycle them?

Anne: I think that ⁶_____ a great idea. Also, any money we make, we can donate to an environmental organisation – like you wanted to, Dan.

Kayla: I totally ⁷_____. Yes, I think this is going to be a great project.

Anne: You can say that ⁸_____!

I can use question tags to check information.

1 Choose the correct option.

1 Your brother isn't very organised, *is he* / *isn't he*?
2 You're Josh, *don't you* / *aren't you*?
3 They forgot to switch off the TV, *did they* / *didn't they*?
4 You'll help us, *won't you* / *aren't you*?
5 Phil and Sue are going out with each other, *aren't they* / *aren't we*?
6 Chiara hasn't got a bike, *hasn't she* / *has she*?

2 Complete the sentences with question tags. Use the auxiliary verbs below.

| ~~can~~ didn't do have isn't will |

1 We can't recycle these, *can we*?
2 You don't like fish, _____?
3 Jake and Will went to the cinema last night, _____?
4 Lisa won't want to help pick up litter, _____?
5 Sorry, I haven't helped much, _____?
6 Your dad is an environmental officer, _____?

3 Complete the sentences with question tags.

1 This traffic jam is really bad, *isn't it*?
2 We'll waste a lot of water by taking baths, _____?
3 Sara hasn't completed the survey, _____?
4 They didn't use to work at the recycling centre, _____?
5 You recycle all your plastic bags, _____?
6 There were lots of people at the event, _____?

4 Use the prompts to write sentences with question tags.

1 you / like / study / the environment / don't / ?
You like studying the environment, don't you?
2 you / Suzanna / aren't / ?
_____
3 we / recycle / this plastic / can / ?
_____
4 they / like / the film / didn't / ?
_____
5 he / not remember / put out / the recycling bin / did / ?
_____

5 Choose the correct answers.

Carla: It's this building here, [1]___?
Mike: Um, yes – the one that says 'recycling centre'. You can read, [2]___?
Carla: Ha, ha! Very funny. You're a real comedian, [3]___? OK. Here we are. You can take this box, [4]___?
Mike: Sure. Oh, it's quite heavy, [5]___? Don't worry though, I can manage.
Carla: Um, these go in with paper, [6]___?
Mike: That's right – just throw them in. Now where are all the aluminium cans? You didn't forget to bring them, [7]___?
Carla: Oh no! Sorry. I've got such a bad memory, [8]___?
Mike: Ha! Don't worry. I'll bring them round later. Actually, you come past here on your way to school, [9]___?
Carla: That's right. OK, I'll bring them here tomorrow.

1 **(a)** isn't it   **b** is it
   c aren't they   **d** are they
2 **a** don't you   **b** do you
   c can you   **d** can't you
3 **a** do you   **b** are you
   c aren't you   **d** didn't you
4 **a** can you   **b** can't you
   c do you   **d** did you
5 **a** is it   **b** isn't it
   c can it   **d** aren't they
6 **a** don't they   **b** do they
   c can't they   **d** aren't they
7 **a** did you   **b** don't you
   c didn't you   **d** do you
8 **a** don't I   **b** have I
   c got I   **d** haven't I
9 **a** don't you   **b** do you
   c come you   **d** won't you

For each learning objective, tick (✓) the box that best matches your ability.

☺☺ = I understand and can help a friend.　　☹ = I understand but have some questions.

☺ = I understand and can do it by myself.　　☹☹ = I do not understand.

		☺☺	☺	☹	☹☹	Need help?	Now try ...
2.1	Vocabulary					Students' Book pp. 22–23 Workbook pp. 18–19	Ex. 1–2, p. 27
2.2	Grammar					Students' Book p. 24 Workbook p. 20	Ex. 3, p. 27
2.3	Reading					Students' Book p. 25 Workbook p. 21	
2.4	Grammar					Students' Book p. 26 Workbook p. 22	Ex. 4, p. 27
2.5	Listening					Students' Book p. 27 Workbook p. 23	
2.6	Speaking					Students' Book p. 28 Workbook p. 24	Ex. 6, p. 27
2.7	English in use					Students' Book p. 29 Workbook p. 25	Ex. 5, p. 27

2.1 I can talk about pollution and the environment.
2.2 I can talk about past events using the Past Perfect.
2.3 I can understand the main points and identify specific detail in an article.
2.4 I can talk about repeated past actions that no longer happen.
2.5 I can identify specific details in short dialogues.
2.6 I can agree and disagree with other people's point of view.
2.7 I can use question tags to check information.

What can you remember from this unit?

New words I learned (the words you most want to remember from this unit)	**Expressions and phrases I liked** (any expressions or phrases you think sound nice, useful or funny)	**English I heard or read outside class** (e.g. from websites, books, adverts, films, music)

Vocabulary

1 Complete the words in the sentences.

1 Local residents have complained about plans to build a new **f** _ _ _ _ _ _ in the area.

2 After the fire, there was a lot of thick **s** _ _ _ _ in the air.

3 This new green car will **p** _ _ _ _ _ _ the environment less than traditional petrol cars.

4 There was very little rain this summer, which **d** _ _ _ _ _ _ lots of plants in the area.

5 This is a modern **p** _ _ _ _ _ **s** _ _ _ _ _ _ _ where they also sell green fuels for cars.

2 Choose a word from A and a word from B to complete the sentences.

A		B	
climate	endangered	animals	away
public	renewable	change	energy
throw		transport	

1 I can't believe how much stuff people _____! We need to recycle as much as we can.

2 The World Wildlife Fund (WWF) is an organisation which works to protect _____.

3 Many scientists now agree that _____ is the biggest problem in the world today.

4 My parents use _____ every day to go to work and I ride my bike to school.

5 Costa Rica used 99 percent _____ in 2015.

Grammar

3 Complete the text with the Past Perfect form of the verbs below.

> be   collect   do   drop   get up   organise   sign up

On Sunday evening I was very tired because I ¹_____ at five that morning! My friends ²_____ a trip to the park to clean up the litter and I ³_____ for it. When we got there, we realised there ⁴_____ a huge party there the night before because it was an absolute mess! We couldn't believe what those people ⁵_____ to our park. They ⁶_____ hundreds of aluminium cans on the ground and there were plastic bags everywhere. By the time we finished, we ⁷_____ over fifty bags of rubbish!

4 Complete the sentences with the correct form of *used to* and the verbs in brackets.

1 I _____ (play) video games all the time when I was young, but I don't have time now.

2 Sally _____ (not live) here.

3 James and Anna _____ (recycle) a lot less than they do now.

4 A: _____ (Hannah/go) to school by bus?
   B: Yes, she _____.

5 We _____ (not have) a recycling centre in our town.

6 A: _____ (Luke/be) a member of the Clean Up Our Town campaign?
   B: No, he _____.

5 Use the prompts to write sentences with question tags.

1 you / not like / tea / you / ?
   _____

2 plastic bags / pollute / the ocean / they / ?
   _____

3 they / not used to recycle / they / ?
   _____

4 we / forgot / to switch off / the lights / we / ?
   _____

5 climate change / be / a big problem / it / ?
   _____

6 the government / will not / do enough / they / ?
   _____

Speaking language practice

6 Complete the dialogues with one word in each gap.

1 A: I don't think climate change is real.
   B: I _____ disagree!

2 A: This environmental project is brilliant.
   B: You can _____ that again!

3 A: I don't think this is going to work.
   B: Really? I don't _____.

4 A: I think our idea is going to work.
   B: Yes, I suppose _____.

5 A: I think everyone can do more to protect the environment.
   B: I'm not so _____ about that.

1 Match 1–6 with a–f to make phrases from the text.

1 | f | renewable   a   change
2 | ☐ | carbon dioxide   b   resources
3 | ☐ | climate   c   turbines
4 | ☐ | natural   d   emissions
5 | ☐ | wind   e   leader
6 | ☐ | world   f   energy

2 Complete the sentences with the phrases from Exercise 1.

1 Solar and wind power are _renewable energy_.
2 They don't produce _____ which damage the environment.
3 The UK is the _____ in offshore wind farms.
4 _____ is a result of the increase in CO_2 in the atmosphere.
5 _____ include our water and air, and we shouldn't destroy them.
6 _____ are now part of the landscape in many countries.

3 Complete the sentences with the Past Perfect or *used to* form of the verbs in brackets.

1 Britain's electricity _used to come_ (come) from coal and natural gas.
2 There _____ (not be) offshore wind turbines in the UK until recently.
3 I _____ (not understand) the importance of wind power before reading this text.
4 Before they developed wind power, the British _____ (depend) on nuclear power stations.
5 Before 2005, the UK _____ (not open) any wind power farms – now they are everywhere.

4 Choose the correct option.

1 We don't think about electricity when we (switch)/ *light* on the kettle in the morning.
2 We take it for *given* / *granted* that we will always have electricity.
3 Unfortunately, we are moving towards a power *supply* / *crisis*.
4 The National Grid is *powered* / *controlled* by twenty-five people.
5 300 power stations create our *precise* / *precious* electricity.
6 High voltage *cables* / *kettles* send energy to our homes.

5 Complete the text with the verbs below.

> close   generate   ~~meet~~   reach   supply

At the moment the National Grid can [1]_meet_ the demands of Britain's users. Nuclear power stations [2]_____ a lot of electricity, but these stations will soon [3]_____ the end of their lives. To make a reduction in CO_2 emissions, the UK government has to hit ambitious targets. To do this, they need to [4]_____ most coal power stations. The secret is to [5]_____ UK homes with renewable energy.

6 Order the words to make sentences.

1 pumping / out / showers / hot water / are
Showers are pumping out hot water.
2 in the country / at / all the electricity / the National Grid / is controlled

_____

3 uses / Britain / of electricity / in winter, / fifty gigawatts

_____

4 to meet / have / might not / enough electricity / all our needs / the National Grid

_____

7 Match sentences 1–4 from Exercise 6 with photos A–D from the video.

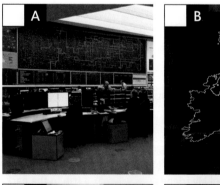
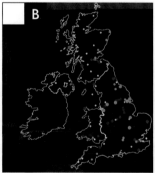
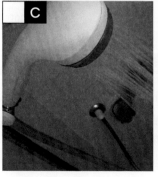
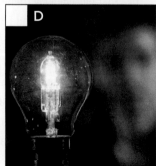

8 Read the video script. Underline any words or phrases you don't know and find their meaning in your dictionary.

Part 1: A power crisis

Every time we switch on a kettle to make some tea or turn on
the heating, we expect our electricity supply to work. We take it
for granted that it will light our houses, cook our food, run our
5 businesses and keep us alive. But in our lifetimes, this electricity
supply could run out. We are quickly moving towards a power crisis.
The nightmare scenario is if our demand for electricity can no
longer be met by our ability to supply it, then the lights go out.
In today's programme, we're investigating this very real problem.
10 We're here at the National Grid to find out how they are dealing
with our increasing demand for energy.
Breakfast time in Britain. The toasters are on, the kettles are boiling
and showers are pumping out hot water. All this requires electricity
and all the electricity in the country is controlled here by this team
15 of twenty-five people. This is the National Grid Control Centre.
Up there on that board you've got every single power station in the
country and the demand at this precise moment.
Over three hundred power stations across the country turn coal,
gas, nuclear and wind into precious electricity. And it's the job of
20 these guys to send that electricity from where it's made to where
we need it – down thousands of miles of high voltage cable, across
the country and directly into our homes. And on this particular
cold winter morning, the demand for electricity is very high, nearly
doubling in just ninety minutes!

Part 2: The future of our power supply

In winter, Britain uses on average fifty gigawatts of electricity –
that's fifty billion watts! The National Grid meets that demand using
seven gigawatts from nine nuclear power stations. Coal power
stations generate around twenty-five gigawatts, gas power stations
make a little more and renewables, including wind, provide around
ten gigawatts. Another six gigawatts comes from abroad or other
sources.
At the moment, the grid has more than enough power to supply all
our needs but over the next ten or twenty years that will change.
The government have set ambitious carbon reduction targets, at
least thirty-four percent fewer carbon emissions by 2020. To hit that
target we have to close almost all our coal power stations and as
our nuclear stations reach the end of their lives, almost all will need
to be switched off too.
So, within ten years the team at the National Grid might not have
enough electricity to meet all our needs. We might not be able to
boil the kettle for tea! And that could be catastrophic, at least for
the British!

3

Style challenge!

VOCABULARY
Clothes and accessories | Adjectives to describe clothes and accessories | *have, be, wear* | Parts of clothes and shoes | Descriptive adjectives

GRAMMAR
Present Perfect Continuous | Present Perfect Simple and Continuous

READING
True or false

LISTENING
Listening for the main points in an interview

SPEAKING
Giving compliments

WRITING
An email

BBC CULTURE
Who is the queen of fashion?

EXAM TIME 1 > p. 114

3.1 **VOCABULARY** Clothes and appearance

I can talk about clothes, accessories and appearance.

1 ● Write the words below in the correct column.

~~boots~~ bracelet earrings gloves hoodie leggings necklace pullover raincoat sandals scarf suit tights tracksuit wellies

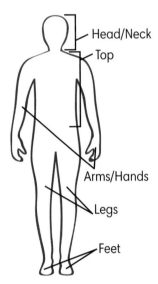

Head/Neck
Top
Arms/Hands
Legs
Feet

Hands/Arms	Top
_____	_____
_____	_____
Legs	**Feet**
_____	*boots*
_____	_____
Head/Neck	**Whole body**
_____	_____
_____	_____
_____	_____

2 ●● Write the correct word from Exercise 1 for each definition.

1 You wear these on your feet in the summer.   *sandals*
2 This is in two parts and you wear it for sport.   _____
3 You need these on your feet in the countryside when it's raining.   _____
4 This is a piece of jewellery around your wrist.   _____
5 These are tight and you wear them on your legs.   _____
6 These keep your hands warm in winter.   _____

3 ●● Choose an adjective from box A and a word from box B to describe the photos. There is one extra word in each box.

A | baggy flowery leather old-fashioned ~~smart~~ striped

B | boots hoodie leggings ~~suit~~ tracksuit tights

1 a *smart suit*   2 an _____   3 a _____

4 _____   5 _____

4 ●● Order the adjectives in brackets.

1 Jill has some *old-fashioned, plain, black* wellies.
(plain / black / old-fashioned)

2 Will is wearing a(n) _____
_____ scarf.
(black-and-white / awesome / checked)

3 Mike hates his _____
_____ tracksuit.
(worn-out / green / baggy)

4 Can you bring my _____
_____ leggings?
(striped / skinny / cotton)

5 Katy loves wearing _____
_____ gloves.
(leather / fashionable / tight)

5 ● **WORD FRIENDS** Complete the sentences with the correct form of *be*, *have* or *wear*.

1 Katie *has* freckles on her face.

2 I think Richard _____ in his twenties.

3 Does your gran _____ a wig?

4 Sally _____ glasses, but only for reading.

5 I _____ a pale complexion and brown hair.

6 Jamie _____ very good-looking!

7 I _____ very slim and tanned in this photo.

8 Last year I wanted to _____ a piercing, but I'm glad I didn't.

6 ●● Complete the sentences with the correct form of *be*, *have* or *wear*. Then choose the correct option.

1 In this picture, Samantha is wearing (*checked, black-and-white*)/ *black-and-white, checked* tights. She *has* a pale complexion.

2 John is in his *teens* / *teenagers* and _____ very good-looking.

3 My dad always wears a smart, plain *tracksuit* / *suit* to work and he never _____ jewellery.

4 Does your sister _____ *dyed* / *died* hair and _____ *fashionable* / *skinny* earrings?

5 Look at this awful *flowery, woollen* / *woollen, flowery* pullover! You'd have to _____ sixty years old to wear this!

7 ●●● Complete the words in the descriptions.

Kylie

My cousin Kylie is very active. She runs every day and plays lots of sport. She's wearing running shoes, [1]s *k i n n y*, [2]p___ -d___ leggings and a baggy [3]h_____.
I don't think I've ever seen her wear clothes not made for sport! When she isn't dressed for running, she wears an old, [4]w_____ -o___ tracksuit at home. You can tell she does a lot of sport outdoors though. She's very [5]s____ and [6]t_____.

Joel

My uncle Joel works in an investment company, so he dresses well for work. He always wears a [7]s_____ suit to work and he [8]w_____ glasses. He has lots of [9]f_____ and a [10]p____ complexion, but I think he's very [11]g____ -l_____.

Amanda

My cousin Amanda is in her teens. She wears [12]s_____ clothes like old [13]j_____ and a baggy [14]p_____. She has [15]d____ hair and she [16]w_____ a lot of jewellery – [17]e_____, necklaces and [18]b_____!

I can talk about things that started in the past and have continued until now.

1 ● Complete the sentences with the Present Perfect Continuous form of the verbs in brackets.

1 Josy really needs to relax. She*'s been revising* (revise) for her test all day.
2 How long _____ (you/wear) my hoodie?
3 Julia _____ (not write) her blog lately.
4 You're late! We _____ (wait) since six!
5 How long _____ (they/collect) vintage fashion magazines?
6 Ian _____ (listen) to this CD for days!

2 ● Complete the table with the phrases below.

| a long time afternoon ages day February four months I got home last Tuesday morning night three hours two o'clock |

for	*since*	*all*
a long time	_____	_____
_____	_____	_____
_____	_____	_____

3 ●● Complete the sentences with the Present Perfect Continuous form of the verbs below.

| feel make not practise walk ~~wear~~ |

1 I *'ve been wearing* glasses for four months.
2 Em _____ the piano much recently.
3 How long _____ (Lucy) nervous about her exams?
4 I'm tired! We _____ round the shops for hours now!
5 How long _____ (you) your own clothes?

4 ●● Complete the second sentence so it has the same meaning as the first one, using the word in brackets. Use between three and five words.

1 We started studying at 4 p.m. It's now 7 p.m. We've *been studying for three* hours. (for)
2 Sara moved here in January. She lives here now. Sara _____ January. (since)
3 What did you do from 9 a.m. until now? What _____ all morning? (doing)
4 Tom didn't do his homework every day last week or this week. Tom _____ his homework recently. (been)
5 They started trying on clothes at 10 a.m. and it's 2 p.m. now! They've been _____! (ages)

5 ●● Find and correct the mistakes in the sentences.

1 You've been wearing the same hoodie since ages!
   for
2 How long you have been waiting?
   _____
3 I haven't doing much exercise recently.
   _____
4 Our neighbours have been playing loud music all of night!
   _____
5 Hurry up! They're waiting for us for ages!
   _____

6 ●●● Complete the text with one word in each gap.

I never used to be interested in my appearance, but recently I've been [1]*wearing* more fashionable clothes. It all started a few weeks ago, when my friend Jana saw me at school and said, 'Kate, you've been coming to school in the same clothes [2]_____ ages now. Let's go shopping together.' I agreed because she was right — I have [3]_____ been shopping for clothes [4]_____ last year, and I really needed some new things.

Now I'm really into fashion and I [5]_____ been writing a blog about new styles [6]_____ the last six months. People tell me they've [7]_____ enjoying it and I get messages from people all over the world. One person asked me, 'How [8]_____ have you been writing the blog?' and couldn't believe it when I told her only six months. She thinks I've been studying fashion [9]_____ my life!

7 Complete the sentences with the words below.

| great last thinking up |

1 Hurry _____! We're going to miss the train!
2 Listen, I've been _____. Why don't you stay with us?
3 Don't worry about the competition. You'll be _____.
4 Nathan! At _____! We've been waiting for ages!

I can identify specific detail in a text.

1 Read the article and choose the best summary.

a Selfies are old-fashioned.

b If you want to succeed, you have to take selfies.

c Selfies are fun, but they should come with a warning label.

The rise and rise of the selfie

What do you do when you've bought some awesome new clothes? Do you show your friends? How about strangers? Why not post a 'selfie' online? It's a great way to get 'likes' from people you've never met, after all.

Every year the *Oxford English Dictionary* publishes a list of the new words it adds to the dictionary and recently, one of those was 'selfie'. People have been taking so many selfies that it's actually become a normal part of our everyday lives. According to a recent survey, the third most common hashtag on social media is *#me*. Walk around any famous place in your city and you'll see people taking selfies in front of famous buildings and statues, instead of just taking a photo of the building or statue.

Some teenagers have a huge following from just taking selfies. Alvin Ritchie, a good-looking teenager from Miami, has a social media page with only his selfies. He has over 90,000 followers! However, this fame hasn't gone to his head. As his profile says, he's just 'a kid who takes photos'.

But it isn't always just harmless fun. A few years ago, Hailey Prescott, a teenager from New Zealand, posted selfies of herself wearing fashionable clothes and the photos went viral. She quickly gained over a million followers and soon after she received offers of modelling contracts in New York.

She became very unhappy though. She felt as if she was living a lie because her photos didn't reflect her true personality. She was eating unhealthily just to look good for her photos. Looking at one photo of her in tight leggings and a baggy T-shirt, she said that the photo was the only thing that made her happy that day. When she realised that her photos were influencing other teenage girls, she decided to stop. She has been making videos since that time to warn other people of the dangers of becoming popular because of how you look.

So the message is clear. Selfies are popular, even normal, and a lot of fun. But who you are will always be more important than what you look like.

2 Read the article again. Mark the sentences T (true) or F (false).

1 ☐ The author thinks you shouldn't post selfies of new clothes.

2 ☐ One of the most popular hashtags on social media is *#me*.

3 ☐ You can see people taking selfies everywhere these days.

4 ☐ Alvin Ritchie thinks he's very important because he's famous.

5 ☐ Hailey Prescott gained a million followers from her modelling contracts.

6 ☐ Posting selfies became more important than eating healthily for Hailey.

7 ☐ The author thinks appearance is the most important thing.

3 Find words or phrases in the article with the meanings below. The words appear in the same order as the sentences.

1 a word or phrase used on social media to identify the topic _hashtag_

2 a lot of people who read your social media posts _____

3 made him feel very important _____

4 not dangerous _____

5 got or received _____

6 pretending to be something you're not _____

I can understand the difference between the Present Perfect Simple and Continuous.

1 ● Match 1–6 with a–f to make sentences.

1 b Alexa has bought a
2 ☐ We've been planning
3 ☐ Mum and Dad have told
4 ☐ I've made
5 ☐ John and Sarah have known
6 ☐ Tom has been wearing

a each other since primary school.
b wig for the party.
c me to wear smarter clothes.
d a necklace. Do you like it?
e that tracksuit all weekend.
f the fashion show for weeks.

2 ●● Choose the correct option to complete the comments. Then mark the sentences PPS (Present Perfect Simple) or PPC (Present Perfect Continuous).

Gemma Fox: Hi, everyone! Come and celebrate my birthday on Saturday 16 August. I'm having a fancy-dress party, so plan your costume in advance!

1 James Stirling: I 've had / 've been having an old tracksuit for years! I'll come as an athlete from the 2000s. *PPS*

2 Kylie Bishop: My boyfriend Gary *has bought / has been buying* a new suit. Gary, I think you should go as the Prime Minister! _____

3 Sarah Clarkson: In the costume shop now. I *'ve tried / 've been trying* on costumes for an hour and I just can't decide what to wear! _____

4 Claire Watts: How long *have you known / have you been knowing* Gemma, Sarah? See you at the party! _____

5 Harry Knowles: Ugh, I *haven't finished / haven't been finished* all my exams yet and my mum won't let me go. _____

6 Julia Case: I *'ve been looking forward / 've looked forward* to this for ages! Definitely coming! ☺ _____

3 ●● Complete the sentences with the Present Perfect Simple or Present Perfect Continuous form of the verbs in brackets.

1 How long *have you been dyeing* (you/dye) your hair?
2 Ed _____ (look for) a new suit for ages.
3 How long _____ (you/have) those boots?
4 I _____ (not post) anything on social media for weeks.
5 Sally _____ (wear) sandals all summer.

4 ●● Use the prompts to write sentences. Use the Present Perfect Simple or Present Perfect Continuous.

1 I / send / three emails / today
   I've sent three emails today.
2 how long / you / have / dyed hair / ?
   _____
3 Jia / wear / glasses / January
   _____
4 how long / you / study / fashion / ?
   _____
5 Mark and Jill / like / heavy metal music / years
   _____

5 ●●● Complete the text with the Present Perfect Simple or Present Perfect Continuous form of the verbs below.

| be   ~~buy~~   make   recycle   send   use   wear

Action Point Clothing

You ¹*'ve bought* a new jacket because you ² _____ your old one for years. Do you throw your old jacket away or take it to a charity shop?

Action Point Clothing in south London has the answer. They ³ _____ old clothes for years. They ⁴ _____ over 200 new items of clothing by transforming old clothes into modern ones. What's more, they ⁵ _____ half of their profits to train young people to design clothes.

So how does it work? 'We started off with a fashion design competition for young people and then used the winning designs on the clothes we received to make them fashionable again,' says company CEO Laura Bauer. 'Since then, there ⁶ _____ no shortage of new designs. The people at our school ⁷ _____ us new designs every week!'

I can identify specific detail in a conversation.

1 Use the picture clues to complete the crossword with parts of clothes.

Across

3  **4**  **6**

7

Down

1 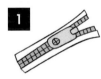 **2** **4**

5 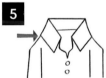 **6**

2 Complete the sentences with words from Exercise 1.

1 Mum, can you help me do up this dress? I think the <u>zip</u> is stuck.

2 Put your _____ up – it's raining.

3 These shoes are so worn-out, I have a hole in the _____ .

4 These _____ are so high that my shoes make me taller than my brother!

5 I really like this shirt, but the _____ are too long. They come all the way over my hands.

6 Can you carry my phone for me, please? My dress hasn't got a _____ .

3 🔊 06 Listen to Jo talking to her mum. Put pictures A–D in the order Jo and her mum talk about them.

4 🔊 06 Listen again. Choose the correct answers.

1 Jo's mum has found
   a some old clothes.
   b something which is interesting to look at.
   c some boxes.

2 What does Jo's mum say about denim shirts in the 1990s?
   a They were popular.
   b They were smart.
   c You had to wear them with jeans.

3 What does Jo's mum say about the 'choker'?
   a It was a type of jewellery.
   b It was very uncomfortable.
   c It was a type of earring.

4 Jo likes
   a her mum's clothes.
   b her dad's shorts.
   c her aunt's clothes.

5 Jo's aunt Emma had
   a lots of friends.
   b beads in her hair.
   c lots of freckles.

I can give and respond to compliments.

1 Complete the phrases with the words below.

brilliant   ~~look~~   really   so   style   suits   taste   what

1   You *look* great in that shirt.
2   You did _____ well.
3   _____ a nice bracelet!
4   You're always _____ helpful.
5   It really _____ you.
6   You've got great _____ in clothes.
7   You were _____ .
8   I like your _____ .

2 Write the phrases from Exercise 1 in the correct column.

Complimenting appearance	Complimenting actions
You look great in that shirt.	_____
_____	_____
_____	_____
_____	

3 Choose the correct option.

1   A: I like what you're wearing today.
      B: That's really (nice) / *brilliant* of you.
2   A: You were amazing.
      B: Thanks, you've *made* / *done* my day.
3   A: You've got great taste in clothes.
      B: Do you really think *so* / *it*?
4   A: You're always so kind.
      B: Oh, thanks. You've made me *be* / *feel* really good.
5   A: Your jacket is awesome.
      B: Are you *know* / *sure*? I don't know if I really like it.

4 Complete the dialogues with one word in each gap.

1   A: James is a bit of a big
            _____ .
      B: I know. He always tells everyone how brilliant he is.
2   A: I just said something really awful to Sandra.
      B: Really? That's not _____ you. You're usually so kind.

5 🔊 07 Complete the dialogues with one word in each gap. Listen and check.

1
Katie: What do you think about this dress, Liz?
Liz: I love it! You [1]*look* great in that colour.
Katie: Do you [2]_____ think so? I'm not sure I like the pockets on the side.
Liz: I see what you mean, but it really [3]_____ you, I think.
Katie: Oh, thanks, Liz. That's really [4]_____ of you. Oh, look at these. [5]_____ nice boots! Why don't you try them on?
Liz: OK. What do you think?
Katie: Those boots [6]_____ awesome! You look great [7]_____ them.
Liz: Oh, thanks. You've got great [8]_____ in clothes.
Katie: Thanks. You've made my [9]_____ . I love going shopping with you!

2
Nick: What a game! I can't believe we won! You [10]_____ brilliant, Jamie.
Jamie: Really? Thanks. You [11]_____ really well too. That goal you scored was amazing!
Nick: Thanks! You've made me [12]_____ really good. Let's celebrate!
Jamie: Yes, let's get a pizza on the way home.

I can write an email with an interesting description.

1 **Choose the adjective which does NOT fit in each sentence.**

1 I love Sara's new ___ skirt.
   a short   b mini   ⓒ handsome

2 Michael likes to think he's quite ___, but everyone just thinks he looks silly.
   a huge   b trendy   c cool

3 I love my cousin. She's really ___.
   a friendly   b baggy   c interesting

4 My mum bought me this ___ shirt.
   a latest   b blue and green striped
   c polka-dot

5 Wow! I love your ___ necklace!
   a bright green   b plastic   c short

2 **Complete the sentences with *so* or *so that*.**

1 Julie is going to a fancy dress party, *so* she needs to make a costume.

2 I'm washing your clothes this evening _____ they'll be ready in the morning.

3 I write a fashion blog _____ I can share my ideas with the world.

4 I want to be a fashion journalist, _____ I'm practising by writing a fashion blog.

5 Mark can't see very well, _____ he wears glasses.

3 **Read Stuart's email to his friend Louis. What is interesting about the school play?**

a There are professional actors involved.

b It's a modern version of an old story.

c It's outside.

Hi Louis,

¹*What have you been up to*? ² _____ , but I've been busy preparing for our school play next month. We're putting on *The Wizard of Oz*. All the music in it will be hip-hop! Guess who I'm going to be! The cowardly lion! I've got an amazing costume. ³ _____ , but it's really baggy, and I'm going to wear some necklaces and bracelets, so I look like a trendy rapper. ⁴ _____ and wear a black-and-white striped cap backwards. Sounds cool, right?

⁵ _____ , I'm allowed to give away two free tickets to the show. So bring your girlfriend and come and watch me. It'll be a lot of fun, I promise!

Anyway, ⁶ _____ . It will be great if you can.

⁷ _____ ,

Stuart

4 **Complete Stuart's email with phrases a–g.**

a I'm going to have a crazy hairstyle

b Sorry I didn't write sooner

c let me know if you can come

d I'm going to wear a lion suit

e Bye for now

f By the way

g What have you been up to

5 **Match 1–5 with a–e to make sentences.**

1 [c] You should see Jane – she's

2 [ ] Write

3 [ ] I've got some

4 [ ] I haven't heard

5 [ ] I also wanted

a from you for ages.

b great news!

c stunning in her new dress.

d to tell you about my holiday.

e back soon.

6 **Complete Charlotte's notes about her school play with the words below.**

| character   ~~invite~~   musical   necklace
| polka-dot   songs   sooner   to come and see

email Sandra to ¹*invite* her to school play
apologise for not writing ² _____
tell her about school ³ _____ :
'Mamma Mia'!
my part: Donna, friend of Sophie, the
main ⁴ _____
costume: ⁵ _____ dress, trendy shoes,
⁶ _____ and bracelets
music: singing Abba ⁷ _____
ask Sandra ⁸ _____ it

7 **Look at the notes in Exercise 6. Write Charlotte's email to Sandra. Follow the instructions below:**

1 Use the email in Exercise 3 as a model.

2 Write three paragraphs:
   - Describe the musical.
   - Describe what you're going to wear.
   - Ask your friend to come and see you.

3 Use words/phrases from Exercises 4–6.

3.8 SELF-ASSESSMENT

😊😊 = I understand and can help a friend.   ☹ = I understand but have some questions.

😊 = I understand and can do it by myself.   ☹☹ = I do not understand.

		😊😊	😊	☹	☹☹	Need help?	Now try ...
3.1	Vocabulary					Students' Book pp. 34–35 Workbook pp. 30–31	Ex. 1–2, p. 39
3.2	Grammar					Students' Book p. 36 Workbook p. 32	Ex. 3, p. 39
3.3	Reading					Students' Book p. 37 Workbook p. 33	
3.4	Grammar					Students' Book p. 38 Workbook p. 34	Ex. 4–5, p. 39
3.5	Listening					Students' Book p. 39 Workbook p. 35	
3.6	Speaking					Students' Book p. 40 Workbook p. 36	Ex. 6, p. 39
3.7	Writing					Students' Book p. 41 Workbook p. 37	

3.1   I can talk about clothes, accessories and appearance.
3.2   I can talk about things that started in the past and have continued until now.
3.3   I can identify specific detail in a text.
3.4   I can understand the difference between the Present Perfect Simple and Continuous.
3.5   I can identify specific detail in a conversation.
3.6   I can give and respond to compliments.
3.7   I can write an email with an interesting description.

What can you remember from this unit?

New words I learned (the words you most want to remember from this unit)	**Expressions and phrases I liked** (any expressions or phrases you think sound nice, useful or funny)	**English I heard or read outside class** (e.g. from websites, books, adverts, films, music)

Vocabulary

1 Complete the sentences with the words below.

> button   gloves   pale   scruffy   tracksuit   wellies

1 Put your _____ on. It's really cold outside and you don't want your hands to freeze.

2 James needs to buy some new clothes. The ones he's wearing look really old and _____ .

3 When you come to the farm, bring a pair of _____ – it gets really muddy.

4 I can't wear this shirt because a _____ has fallen off it.

5 I don't like this shirt – it's too dark. I prefer _____ colours.

6 You need a good _____ if you want to go running in winter.

2 Match words 1–6 with definitions a–f.

1 ☐ appearance
2 ☐ second-hand
3 ☐ dyed
4 ☐ heel
5 ☐ earrings
6 ☐ freckles

a   not its natural colour
b   jewellery you wear on your ears
c   what you look like
d   the bottom, back part of a shoe
e   used, not new
f   small brown dots on your skin

Grammar

3 Complete the sentences with the Present Perfect Continuous form of the verbs in brackets. Then write *for*, *since* or *all*.

1 We _____ (work) hard _____ this morning.

2 Sally _____ (study) English _____ she was seven.

3 Our dog _____ (run) around the garden _____ morning.

4 We _____ (not wait) _____ very long.

5 The neighbours _____ (make) lots of noise _____ hours now!

6 My brother _____ (not write) his blog much _____ last month.

4 Choose the correct option.

1 How long *have you known / have you been knowing* Jim?

2 Julia *has had / has been having* pierced ears since she was fourteen.

3 How long *have you worn / have you been wearing* glasses?

4 I'm so full. *I've eaten / I've been eating* three sandwiches!

5 Hi, James! We *have waited / have been waiting* for you!

5 Complete the text with the Present Perfect Simple or Continuous form of the verbs in brackets.

Clothes and memories

I ^{1}_____ (tidy) my wardrobe and I ^{2}_____ (find) a lot of clothes which have important memories for me. Yesterday I found an old T-shirt which I ^{3}_____ (have) for five years. I ^{4}_____ (grow) a lot since then, so it doesn't fit any more, but I remember wearing it on holiday in Italy one year.

I ^{5}_____ (think) about that holiday a lot since then because we had such a great time. I ^{6}_____ (find) a blanket too. I used to sleep with it when I was little! I must stop now though because I ^{7}_____ (do) this all afternoon, and I ^{8}_____ (not finish) my homework yet!

Speaking language practice

6 Complete the dialogues with one word in each gap.

1 A: What a _____ T-shirt!
   B: Do you really _____ so? I'm not sure I like it.

2 A: You did _____ well today. Well done!
   B: Thanks, that's really _____ of you.

3 A: You _____ fantastic in the game yesterday.
   B: Thanks! You've _____ me feel really good.

4 A: You've _____ great taste in clothes.
   B: Thanks. You've made my _____ !

5 A: You have a _____ smile.
   B: Thanks. You're always _____ kind.

1 Complete the sentences with the phrases below.

> clothes brands   designer fashion   fashion icon
> modern touch   tartan skirt   ~~trendy look~~

1 They created a really _trendy look_ from a very traditional style.
2 The Queen must be the unlikeliest _____ of all time.
3 Dolce and Gabbana produce some of the best _____ in the world.
4 A kilt is a knee-length _____ worn traditionally by men in Scotland.
5 The new design director is using designs from the 1960s, but giving them a _____ .
6 Kate Middleton has helped increase the sales of some UK _____ .

2 Look at the photo and tick (✓) the best descriptions 1–2 below.

1 ☐ She's wearing a headscarf, a tartan skirt, wellies and is carrying a handbag.
2 ☐ She's wearing a headscarf, a tartan dress, shoes and gloves.

3 Rewrite the sentences using the Present Perfect Simple or Present Perfect Continuous form of the verbs in brackets. Use _for_ or _since_ where necessary.

1 British people wore Barbour coats years ago. They are still wearing them today.
   British people have been wearing Barbour
   coats for years. (wear)
2 Burberry tartan was popular in the 1920s. It still is today.
   _____ (be)
3 Dolce and Gabbana started designing clothes together in 1982. They are still designing clothes together today.
   _____ (design)
4 Kate Middleton liked high street fashion when she was a teenager. She still likes it today.
   _____ (like)
5 The 'royal look' is fashionable again, thanks to Kate Middleton.
   _____ (become)

4 Choose the correct option.

1 Classic British fashion designs are based on what (country)/ city people like to wear.
2 Designer clothes look fantastic but unfortunately, they're not trendy / affordable for most people.
3 The Barbour jacket is very distinctive / informal because of the material it is made from.
4 Kate Middleton's look is a(n) extravagant / careful combination of designer fashion and high street brands.
5 These coats have to be affordable / waterproof because of the weather.

5 Match the adjectives below with definitions 1–6.

> ~~award-winning~~   functional   ripped
> state-of-the-art   successful   tough

1 something which has won a prize   _award-winning_
2 doing well, achieving what you want   _____
3 damaged or torn, especially for clothes   _____
4 using the most modern ideas   _____
5 practical and simple in design   _____
6 hard to break or damage   _____

6 Complete the text about British fashion company Barbour with the adjectives from Exercise 5.

Barbour

James Percy designs clothes for Barbour, using [1]_state-of-the-art_ technology and the most modern materials available. He combines these with a very simple and [2]_____ design to create the perfect coat. In fact, it is these jackets that have made Barbour such a(n) [3]_____ company. As style director, James' [4]_____ designs have made Barbour famous not just in Britain, but all over the world.

The material used for Barbour jackets means that they are very [5]_____ and can't easily be damaged. However, some British people like their jackets to look worn-out and even [6]_____ – just like some teenagers like their jeans! Other European customers prefer their jackets to look and feel completely new.

7 Read the video script. Underline any words or phrases you don't know and find their meaning in your dictionary.

Part 1: An unlikely fashion icon

Classic country clothes have always been the uniform of choice for the British upper classes. But they have not always been fashionable. That is changing! There's something about old England and tradition. Many designers think

5 the English have a strange but brilliant sense of style, which is a constant inspiration for them.

This look says something about the people who wear it. It's a status symbol. In fact, the biggest fan of this style is the poshest person of all – the Queen! And she's become an unlikely fashion icon. The Italian fashion designers

10 Dolce and Gabbana recently used her look to create one of their collections. Royal dressing does stand for something in people's eyes all over the world. It stands for things that endure, values that endure.

The genius of traditional British style is that it's perfectly practical. In every garment there's a little bit of the country dream. These clothes are world

15 famous today but the stories behind them are not. Landscape. The weather. War. Class. Nostalgia. The designs have been evolving for generations. Now the same look is being updated for the tastes of today. This is the look that sums up British style – these classic outdoor clothes, designed to protect us from the weather and the outside world.

20 ## Part 2: The Barbour jacket

The one garment that protects British people more than any other is the Barbour jacket. This is Lord James Percy, who is the company's style director. Today Barbour is one of the most successful clothing companies in Britain and Percy has designed many award-winning coats for the brand.

25 James Percy is involved with Barbour in the development of a technical sporting range using state-of-the-art fabric technology alongside functional design.

Barbour have been making their trademark wax jackets for over a century but their sales increased dramatically when a film called *The Queen* showed

30 Her Majesty wearing one behind the wheel of her Land Rover.

The day after the premiere, a lady walked into their store in New York and asked for the jacket that the Queen was wearing in the film. Soon after that, their sales – certainly in New York – had doubled.

Americans may have only just started wearing Barbours, but in Europe they have been wearing these jackets for decades! James Percy knows the jackets and the people who wear them really well.

European customers like their coats to be in perfect condition – brand new and shiny. However, the British like to have their coats look older. It shows that they lived in them for ten, twenty, thirty years. They can be ripped and smelly – the dirtier the better!

This is one way to make your jacket look older!

Look at that! Nice! What else can we do to it?

As you can see, James had a good aim! But the coat is very hard-wearing. The shot hardly even marked it. It isn't bullet-proof but it's unbelievably tough. Now, that should be about right.

4

Team work

VOCABULARY
Jobs | Finding and losing a job |
Working conditions | Success at work

GRAMMAR
Talking about the future |
Future Continuous

READING
Multiple matching

LISTENING
Listening for specific detail

SPEAKING
Instructions and reminders

ENGLISH IN USE
Verbs with prepositions

BBC CULTURE
What is the happiest profession?

I can talk about jobs and work experience.

1 ● Look at the pictures complete the words for jobs.

1 p l u m b e r

2 m _ _ _ _ _ _ _

3 d _ _ _ _ _ _ 's assistant

4 c _ _ _

5 flight
a _ _ _ _ _ _ _ _

6 s _ _ _ _ _ _ _

7 l _ _ _ _ _ _ _ _

8 l _ _ _ _ _ _ _ _

9 film
d _ _ _ _ _ _ _

2 ●● Read what the people are saying and write their jobs. Choose a word from A and a word from B.

A app   fashion   film   flight   lorry   music   ~~travel~~   veterinary

B ~~agent~~   assistant   attendant   critic   designer (x2)   director   driver

> I organise people's summer holidays for them.

1 *travel agent*

> I travel by plane in my job.

2 _____

> I design and create trendy new clothes.

3 _____

> I write programs and games for mobile phones.

4 _____

> I drive big vehicles or trucks over long distances.

5 _____

> I listen to a lot of new music and write reviews.

6 _____

> I help my boss to treat animals which are ill.

7 _____

> I manage the actors and other people involved in making a movie.

8 _____

3 ● **WORD FRIENDS** Match 1–6 with a–f to make sentences.

1 [d] Plumbers need to have
2 [ ] Have you heard about Jack? He got
3 [ ] It's great to be part
4 [ ] Before you start looking for jobs, you need to write
5 [ ] Doctors usually earn
6 [ ] My grandfather doesn't work anymore. He's

a of a team in my job. I learn a lot from my colleagues.
b a good salary.
c a CV.
d training so that they know how to repair things.
e fired for being rude to a customer!
f retired.

4 ●● **WORD FRIENDS** Choose the correct option.

My brother's new job

When my brother finished university, he immediately started ¹(looking for)/ having a job. One day he saw an advert for a job he liked, so he decided to ²look / apply for it. The company liked his CV and they asked him to come in and ³meet / have an interview. A week later, they phoned him and told him he was successful. They asked him to come back the next day to ⁴get / sign a contract and ⁵meet / look for his colleagues. He's been there a week now and really enjoys it. They said that if he works hard, he'll ⁶get / apply for a promotion!

5 ● Choose the correct answers.

1 My boss told me that I'm going to get a pay ___ next month!
   a up   b increase   (c) rise
2 My cousin has a really ___-paid job in the city.
   a good   b well   c hourly
3 You can choose from two ___: 6 a.m.–2 p.m. or 2 p.m.–10 p.m.
   a overtime b shifts   c holidays
4 My dad works for a small ___. They only have four employees.
   a firm   b shift   c bonus
5 Harry had a ___-time job when he was at school, working on Saturdays.
   a full   b part   c temporary
6 In this job you'll get four weeks' paid ___ a year.
   a holiday b bonus   c shift

6 ●● Complete the sentences with the words below. There are two extra words.

> assistant bonus flexible flight ~~lifeguard~~ manager overtime paid pension rate summer wage

1 I love my summer job on the beach as a(n) *lifeguard*, but the hourly _____ is very low.
2 My sister works as a(n) _____ in a big company. She has a team of ten assistants. If she works hard, she gets a huge _____ at the end of the year!
3 Judy has got a(n) _____ job in July and August this year. She's working with animals as a veterinary _____.
4 My mum is a(n) _____ attendant and she has to work a lot of _____. Sometimes I don't see her for three days!
5 My grandparents are retired, so they don't get a(n) _____; they get a(n) _____.

7 ●● Choose the correct option.

1 My uncle is (a psychologist)/ an interpreter. He studies how the mind works, and it's quite a well-paid / an unemployed job.
2 I hope I'm unemployed / retired by the time I'm sixty. I'd like to give up / fired work before I'm too old.
3 Last year my sister was permanent / unemployed. While she was looking for a job, she got unemployment benefit / pension.
4 When I leave school, I'd like to work as a computer programmer / attendant and work flexible hours / overtime.
5 My mum works shifts / hourly as a dentist's assistant / agent.

8 ●● Complete the text with one word in each gap.

My cousin works as a ¹m*anager* in a computer ²c_____. It's a ³w_____-p_____ job and he ⁴e_____ a good salary. If he does well, he gets a big ⁵b_____ at the end of the year. Recently he got a ⁶p_____. He got a bigger office and a big ⁷p_____ r_____, but now he has to work lots of ⁸o_____; sometimes he doesn't finish work till 9 p.m. But his dream is to work in the music industry – he wants to become a ⁹m_____ c_____. He's been looking ¹⁰f_____ a job but it's really difficult. First you have to gain a lot of work ¹¹e_____, but he can't do that in his current job. He's determined to follow his dream. He even joked once that he wants to get ¹²f_____ so he can go and do it!

I can use different tenses to talk about future events.

1 ● Order the words to make sentences.

1 going / next year / I'm / get / a pay rise / to
I'm going to get a pay rise next year.

2 starts / 7 September / on / the training

_____

3 Jake / a diploma / next year / going / is / study / to / for

_____

4 if / the job / really boring / you / it's / enjoy / won't

_____

5 the manager / meeting / eleven o'clock / we're / at

_____

6 a CV / want / I'll / write / you / help / you / if

_____

_____

7 some money / earn / able / this summer / I'll / to / be

_____

_____

2 ● Choose the correct option.

1 Naomi was rude to several customers and she (*is going to get*)/ *will get* fired from her job at the café!

2 We need to hurry – the lesson *starts* / *will start* in ten minutes.

3 I don't think Sally *will get* / *is getting* the job working at summer camp. She doesn't have enough experience.

4 I don't know how to prepare for the job interview. *Will* / *Do* you help me?

5 I *will meet* / *am meeting* Ann for lunch at noon tomorrow.

6 I *look* / *am going to look* for a part-time job next month.

3 ●● Complete the text messages with the correct form of the verbs in brackets.

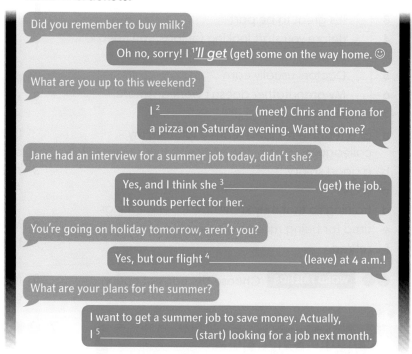

Did you remember to buy milk?

Oh no, sorry! I ¹*'ll get* (get) some on the way home. ☺

What are you up to this weekend?

I ² _____ (meet) Chris and Fiona for a pizza on Saturday evening. Want to come?

Jane had an interview for a summer job today, didn't she?

Yes, and I think she ³ _____ (get) the job. It sounds perfect for her.

You're going on holiday tomorrow, aren't you?

Yes, but our flight ⁴ _____ (leave) at 4 a.m.!

What are your plans for the summer?

I want to get a summer job to save money. Actually, I ⁵ _____ (start) looking for a job next month.

4 ●●● Read the dialogue. Choose the correct answers.

Paul: Have you got any plans for the summer, Manisha?

Manisha: Not really. I think I ¹___ at home. What about you?

Paul: I ²___ a summer job – it's all arranged.

Manisha: Wow, really? What ³___?

Paul: Well, I ⁴___ at the publishing company my aunt works for – she's an editor there. I can choose whether I want to work in the office or have training as a journalist.

Manisha: So what ⁵___?

Paul: I ⁶___ as a journalist. It will be badly-paid, but I think it ⁷___ more interesting than office work.

Manisha: Definitely! That sounds great, Paul. I'm jealous! You ⁸___ me all about it when you're there.

Paul: Of course! I ⁹___ you on the first day to let you know how I'm getting on.

Manisha: Please do. Oh, is that the time? I should go. My train ¹⁰___ in three minutes! See you!

Paul: Bye, Manisha. Speak soon!

1 ⓐ 'll just relax b 'm just relaxing c just relax

2 a 'm getting b 'll get c get

3 a do you do b will you do c are you going to do

4 a work b 'm working c 'll work

5 a are you doing b do you do c will you do

6 a am going to train b will train c am training

7 a is being b be c will be

8 a 'll must tell b 'll have to tell c 're having to tell

9 a 'm texting b 'll text c 'm going to text

10 a leaves b will leave c can leave

I can find specific detail in short texts.

1 Match words and phrases 1–6 with definitions a–f.

1 [b] opportunity
2 [ ] eye for detail
3 [ ] vacancy
4 [ ] good communicator
5 [ ] physically fit
6 [ ] available

a someone who is able to express ideas clearly
b chance to do something
c a job for someone to do
d ready to start work
e be good at noticing small but important things
f someone who is healthy and strong

2 Read the ads for part-time jobs. Match the jobs below with the ads. There is one extra job.

app tester   children's entertainer   fashion designer
football coach   trainee journalist

A _____ **Put your skills into practice!**

Are you interested in the latest styles? Are you creative and good at art? If so, Walkwise are looking for a young person to create new looks for our teen department. This is a great opportunity to gain experience in the clothing industry. We offer flexible hours and we'll pay you for each design we use. We'll also give you samples of your designs to wear. Call Sue Donaghy on 0207 528 6943 for more details.

B _____ **5-3-2 Magazine**

We are an online football magazine aimed at teenagers and we are looking for someone who wants to be part of our team of content creators. This is a great opportunity for someone with an eye for detail and excellent writing skills. You won't earn much, but you'll gain some really useful experience and work with a team of people who are also football-mad! It's a part-time job, working in our office on Kent's Hill Road. Hours are from 9 a.m. until 3 p.m. on Saturdays. Visit our website at www.532mag.com for information on how to apply.

C _____ **Fairytale Parties: new vacancy**

We're looking for a new party princess (or prince) to provide entertainment at children's parties. You will need to be a good communicator who likes working with children. You will also have to be physically fit because the job involves singing, dancing and acting with groups of very energetic young children. You need to be available to work at weekends. If this sounds like the job for you, send your CV to info@ftparties.com.

D _____ **Exciting opportunity at Zilo Games!**

Are you into technology, creative and do you enjoy playing games on your mobile phone? Would you like to play and test mobile games and get paid for it? This is an exciting part-time job for somebody aged between fourteen and sixteen who loves playing games all the time. You will also have some training in designing apps. If this is for you, then send a description of your favourite game and why you like it in no more than 150 words to zilozilo@zg.com.

3 Three young people are looking for an interesting part-time job. Match the people with ads A–D. There is one extra ad.

[ ] **Lisa**
Lisa loves performing and also plays football for her school team. She usually does a lot of babysitting and is now looking for a new challenge. She's very sociable and loves working with lots of different people.

[ ] **Silvia**
Silvia is seventeen years old. She is very creative and spends a lot of time on her mobile phone, using different types of apps. She's also very good at drawing. She loves shopping for clothes, but needs to get a part-time job so she can buy them.

[ ] **James**
James is really into football and cycling. He also loves playing different types of sports games on his mobile phone and then writing reviews of them in his own blog. His blog is very popular and he spends a lot of time at the weekend writing it.

I can talk about actions in progress in the future.

1 ● Match 1–6 with a–f to make sentences.

1 [c] At 6 p.m. tonight I'll
2 [ ] When will
3 [ ] Harry and Andrew won't be
4 [ ] In twenty
5 [ ] Next summer, Anya
6 [ ] What will you be

a years, I'll be working for a big company.
b doing at 10 p.m. tonight?
c be having dinner with my family.
d will be working at a summer camp.
e Liz be having her interview?
f working here next year.

2 ● Order the words to make sentences.

Shirley Thomas: Yay! The exams are finally over and this time next week I'll be working in an animal shelter. 🐱🐶🐰🐭 What about you? What will you be doing this summer?

1 **Graeme Marks:** In two weeks, _I'll be starting a summer job_ at the beach.
(I'll / a summer job / starting / be)

2 **Julia Somme:** _____
_____ ☹ (going / holiday / we / be / won't / abroad on)

3 **Ritchie Alba:** _____
_____ (my cousin / I'll / in Greece / staying / with / be / !)

4 **Gemma Sykes:** _____
_____ next week, Emma? (celebrating / your birthday / how / be / you / will / ?)

5 **Emma Flynn:** _____
_____ (be / I'll / party / a / having / !)

3 ●● Complete the sentences with one word in each gap.

1 I hope I'll be working with animals _in_ the future.
2 Will you _____ seeing Alice tonight?
3 What will you be doing _____ 10 a.m. tomorrow?
4 They _____ be studying Italian next year because they won't have time.
5 _____ year I'll be starting a new school.
6 In ten years I hope I'll be _____ an interesting job.

4 ●●● Complete the blog post with the Future Continuous form of the verbs below. There are two extra verbs.

| apply design earn gain get have show start ~~study~~ relax |

● ● ●

How I'll get my dream job

I love technology and my dream is to become an app designer. These are the things I think I'll be doing at different times to achieve this dream:

1 This year I _will be studying_ for my exams.
2 In two years I _____ for university.
3 While I'm at university, I _____ my own apps.
4 In five years I _____ job interviews.
5 In ten years I _____ lots of experience in a tech company.
6 In fifteen years I _____ my own company.
7 In twenty years I _____ lots of money. ☺
8 In thirty years I'll retire and I _____ on a beach!

What about you? What's your dream job?

5 Complete the dialogues with phrases a–c.

OUT of **class**

a Just wait and see.
b I've been waiting for ages!
c Do you mind?

1 A: John, I'm ready to go now.
B: At last! _____
2 A: You need to study more.
B: _____ I've been working really hard this week!
3 A: I'm sure you'll do really well on Saturday.
_____
B: Thanks, Jenny. That's really nice of you.

I can understand specific detail in a conversation about future jobs.

1 Use the clues to complete the crossword.

```
          ¹e
    ²c     |
     |     |
     |  ³s |
 ⁴d  i  p  l  o  m  a
     |     |
⁵a _ _ _   |
     |  ⁶c _ _ _ _ _
     |     |
     |     |
     |     |
```

Across

4 At the end of the course you'll receive a *diploma*.

5 My sister has won an _____ for her school project.

6 When I graduate, I'd like to start a successful _____ as a doctor.

Down

1 This _____ pays its staff well and gives them five weeks' paid holiday a year.

2 There were ten _____ at the job interview, but only one was successful.

3 Last week a computer programmer came to our school to give a _____ about his job.

2 🔊 08 Listen to Marcus and Cathy talking about their future. Who do you think will earn more money?

_____

3 🔊 08 Listen again. Mark the sentences T (true) or F (false).

1 ☐ Cathy isn't sure what she wants to do when she's older.

2 ☐ She wants to have a very well-paid job.

3 ☐ Marcus wants to be rich.

4 ☐ He works part-time for a pet shop.

5 ☐ He wants to start a business as soon as he leaves school.

6 ☐ He's going to retire when he's seventy.

7 ☐ Cathy thinks money isn't the only thing to think about.

4 Complete the phrases from the listening with the words below. There is one extra word.

> billionaire   bothered   happens
> impressed   ~~no~~   ready

1 I have *no* idea!

2 I'm not that _____ …

3 As it _____, (I already have my own business).

4 I'm really _____.

5 (I think you'll become) a _____ …

5 Match the phrases from Exercise 4 with their meanings.

a ☐ actually

b ☐ a person with over £1,000,000,000

c ☐ 1 I really don't know

d ☐ I respect and admire what you've done

e ☐ this is not important to me

I can give instructions, remind somebody what to do and respond.

1 Match 1–6 with a–f to make instructions for a cheese and tomato pizza.

1   [b]   First,
2   [ ]   Don't forget
3   [ ]   Put the cheese and tomato on the pizza base. Try not
4   [ ]   Put the pizza in the oven. After a
5   [ ]   That seems
6   [ ]   Then what

a   to spill any tomato over the sides of the pizza.
b   grate the cheese and cut up the tomato.
c   few minutes, take it out again.
d   do I do?
e   easy.
f   to switch on the oven and let it get hot.

2 Complete the dialogues with the words below.

| always   hope   important   last
| remember   ~~secondly~~

1   A: What do I do after that?
    B: _Secondly_, clean the table.
2   A: Can I take my break at any time?
    B: Yes, but _____ to ask if it's OK first.
3   A: It's _____ to be polite to the customers.
    B: Yes, of course.
4   A: And finally, put the dishes away in the cupboard.
    B: OK, I _____ I remember it all!
5   A: Do I take the pizza out of the oven then?
    B: Yes, but _____ use gloves to lift it. It's really hot.
6   A: Is that everything?
    B: Almost. The _____ thing you need to do is switch off the air conditioner.

3 Choose the correct option.

1   Take it out for a few minutes. After (that)/ then, put it back in the oven again.
2   *No / Not* worries. I think I can remember everything.
3   Before you leave, don't *remember / forget* to prepare the orders for the next day.
4   Try *not to / to* get nervous. Just be yourself.
5   *Be / Do* sure to ask how much it costs.
6   *Final / Finally*, put the gloves back in the box.

4 Complete the sentences with the phrases below.

OUT of
class

| he's off sick   it's all very simple

1   Mr Williams isn't in today. _____ , so I'll be teaching you.
2   _____ . You just need to make sure you read the label carefully.

5 🔊 09 Complete the dialogue with one word in each gap. Listen and check.

Claire: Hi, Ian. Nice to meet you. I'm Claire – I'm your manager. Let's get started then. [1]_**First**_, you get changed in here and store your clothes and things in your cupboard. If you arrive early, you can wait and have a drink in the staff canteen.

Ian: [2]_____ worries.

Claire: After [3]_____, come and find me and I'll tell you what you need to do each day.

Ian: OK, great! What jobs will I do today?

Claire: Let's see. Start by looking at the shelves to see which products need replacing. [4]_____ to write them down. Next, go to the storage area at the back of the shop, find the products you need and put them on the shelf.

Ian: That [5]_____ easy.

Claire: Yes, it usually is, except when it gets really busy. The shelves become empty quickly and sometimes a customer might be angry if they can't find an item.

Ian: Oh. [6]_____ what?

Claire: Well, try [7]_____ to get nervous. It's important to [8]_____ polite. Find out what they need and go and find it in the storage area.

Ian: OK. I hope I remember it [9]_____!

Claire: You'll be fine. Any problems, just come and ask me, OK?

I can use a wide range of verbs that are followed by a preposition.

1 Choose the correct option.

1 What are you complaining *on /* *about* now?

2 Yuck! This food smells *of / about* old clothes!

3 Have you prepared *on / for* your job interview?

4 Ssh! I need to concentrate *on / in* my homework!

5 At this school we believe *in / on* dedication and hard work.

6 Can you help me deal *with / for* this problem?

2 Complete the sentences with the prepositions below. Then match the sentences with pictures A–E.

| ~~about~~   for   in   of   on |

1 ☐ C   I'm worried *about* the exam. I haven't studied at all!

2 ☐   Don't worry, Mrs. Atkins. We'll find Timmy. You can depend _____ us.

3 ☐   We specialise _____ antique furniture.

4 ☐   Can I apologise _____ something I'm going to do?

5 ☐   What exactly does this dish consist _____?

3 Write the words below in the correct column.

| apologise   apply   believe   compare   ~~complain~~   concentrate consist   cope   depend   smell   succeed   worry |

about	for	in	of	on	with
complain	_____	_____	_____	_____	_____
_____	_____	_____	_____	_____	_____

4 Find and correct the mistakes in the sentences. One sentence is correct.

1 That company specialises ~~on~~ making birthday cakes.
in

2 The book consists with four parts.
_____

3 Don't worry for picking me up tonight – I'll get the bus.
_____

4 I really can't cope with all my homework this week.
_____

5 You should apologise of what you said.
_____

6 You shouldn't compare yourself about others.
_____

7 If you want to succeed on this class, you'll need to do extra reading.
_____

8 I'm not sure – it depends of the situation.
_____

5 Complete the text with one word in each gap.

Getting ahead

What's the secret to succeeding [1]*in* your life and at school? Some people say it's believing [2]_____ yourself. Others say it's concentrating [3]_____ what you have to do. Recent research suggests that it might, in fact, be … behaving badly! Studytech, a research company that specialises [4]_____ effective study strategies, recently studied the behaviour of hundreds of successful students and discovered that those who argue [5]_____ their classmates and teachers more than usual are those who get good grades. These people rarely or never apologise [6]_____ mistakes they have made and never worry [7]_____ offending other people. They also complain [8]_____ situations loudly when they don't like them. The behaviour of the students interviewed also consisted [9]_____ things like taking the credit for other people's work and arriving late for class. Although they are usually disliked, classmates like the fact that they can depend [10]_____ these people and find they are the best at dealing [11]_____ difficult situations.

For each learning objective, tick (✓) the box that best matches your ability.

☺☺ = I understand and can help a friend.

☺ = I understand and can do it by myself.

☹ = I understand but have some questions.

☹☹ = I do not understand.

		☺☺	☺	☹	☹☹	Need help?	Now try ...
4.1	Vocabulary					Students' Book pp. 46–47 Workbook pp. 42–43	Ex. 1–2, p. 51
4.2	Grammar					Students' Book p. 48 Workbook p. 44	Ex. 3, p. 51
4.3	Reading					Students' Book p. 49 Workbook p. 45	
4.4	Grammar					Students' Book p. 50 Workbook p. 46	Ex. 4, p. 51
4.5	Listening					Students' Book p. 51 Workbook p. 47	
4.6	Speaking					Students' Book p. 52 Workbook p. 48	Ex. 6, p. 51
4.7	English in use					Students' Book p. 53 Workbook p. 49	Ex. 5, p. 51

4.1   I can talk about jobs and work experience.

4.2   I can use different tenses to talk about future events.

4.3   I can find specific detail in short texts.

4.4   I can talk about actions in progress in the future.

4.5   I can understand specific detail in a conversation about future jobs.

4.6   I can give instructions, remind somebody what to do and respond.

4.7   I can use a wide range of verbs that are followed by a preposition.

What can you remember from this unit?

New words I learned (the words you most want to remember from this unit)	**Expressions and phrases I liked** (any expressions or phrases you think sound nice, useful or funny)	**English I heard or read outside class** (e.g. from websites, books, adverts, films, music)

Vocabulary

1 Choose the correct option.

1 James is studying Biology and Chemistry so that he can become a *scientist / computer programmer* when he's older.
2 The *cleaner / manager* usually starts work after everybody has left for the day.
3 My mum works as a *lorry driver / travel agent*, so we get cheap holidays!
4 The new school *lifeguard / cook* is terrible. This food tastes disgusting!
5 Carla's mum is a *fashion designer / dentist's assistant*, so she always wears nice clothes!
6 Tom's dad is a famous *writer / plumber*.

2 Match the words below with definitions 1–6.

> bonus   wage   pension   unemployment benefit
> shift   temporary job

1 money you receive from the government when you haven't got a job _____
2 a regular payment you receive for working _____
3 the time period you work for _____
4 extra money you receive if you work very hard _____
5 a job you do for a fixed/short period of time _____
6 money you receive when you are retired _____

Grammar

3 Complete the dialogues with the correct future form of the verbs in brackets.

1 A: What are you doing tonight?
  B: Not much. I _____ (watch) a film and then go to bed.
2 A: I'm really hungry after that football match.
  B: I _____ (make) you a sandwich if you like.
3 A: Do you think Macy _____ (pass) the exam?
  B: I'm not sure. She hasn't studied much at all.
4 A: What time do we need to leave?
  B: Well, our train _____ (leave) at eleven, so we should leave home at ten.
5 A: Can you come with us tonight?
  B: I _____ (go) to the cinema with my parents – we arranged it last week.

4 Complete the text with the Future Continuous form of the verbs below. There is one extra verb.

> apply   choose   live   move   not do
> study   work

Next year I ¹_____ in New York! My dad has got a new job there, so, we ²_____ there at the end of the year. He ³_____ at the same company, but he ⁴_____ the same job because he's been promoted. I ⁵_____ at a new school too, so I'm hoping I'll make lots of new friends. In a few years I ⁶_____ for universities there too. I'm really excited!

5 Complete the sentences with one preposition in each gap.

1 Jacqueline always complains _____ everything. She's no fun to be around.
2 I'm not sure if I can come out tonight. It depends _____ my mum.
3 The course consists _____ three modules.
4 Do you believe _____ love at first sight?
5 I've applied _____ three summer jobs this year.
6 Please stop arguing _____ your brother.

Speaking language practice

6 Complete the dialogues with the words below. There are two extra words.

> always   few   important   no   sure
> that (x2)   then   remember   to

1 A: After a _____ minutes, add the sauce.
  B: OK.
2 A: It's _____ to stay calm.
  B: I'm trying!
3 A: Be _____ to listen to the customer.
  B: _____ seems easy.
4 A: Don't forget _____ feed the cat.
  B: _____ problem.
5 A: _____ what do I do?
  B: After _____, take the order.

1 Match 1–6 with a–f to make phrases from the text.

1	c fast	a	criteria
2	☐ job	b	factor
3	☐ high	c	results
4	☐ recent	d	status
5	☐ key	e	survey
6	☐ important	f	satisfaction

2 Complete the sentences with the phrases from Exercise 1.

1 There are a lot of *important criteria* to consider when choosing a job.
2 Making customers happy helps to give staff a sense of _____.
3 A _____ in being happy at work is a good relationship with colleagues.
4 Jobs with a _____ might pay well, but they can also be very stressful.
5 A _____ about happiness at work came to some surprising conclusions.
6 Some workers get very _____ in their jobs – they can see what they have achieved straightaway.

3 Order the words to make sentences.

1 on their skills / two experts / are / judge / the contestants / going to
   Two experts are going to judge the contestants on their skills.
2 be / the young hairdressers / designing / which the judges request / will / the styles
   _____
3 going / Lisa / to / what she does best / – hair / is / do / !
   _____
4 stand out / thinks / will / from the others / Becky / she
   _____
5 will / to / only one person / claim / be able / the title
   _____
6 the best / which girl / the judges / convince / that she is / will / ?
   _____

4 Choose the correct option.

1 The contestants are putting the (finishing)/ perfect touches to their hairstyles.
2 Which one will be the *proud / winning* look?
3 Now is the moment of *decision / truth*!

4 Both girls want to claim the *title / winner* of Young Hairdresser of the Year.
5 But can Becky prove that she's *top / number* one in her profession?
6 Becky can't believe the *last / final* result!

5 Complete the text with the words below.

| ~~distinct~~ entire final proud tough |

The contest encouraged the candidates to create [1]*distinct* hairstyles – something truly original. In the final part, the two candidates had to create an [2]_____ look – hair, make-up, clothes and shoes. It's a really [3]_____ challenge! For the judges, it was a difficult decision to make, but in the end they agreed on their [4]_____ verdict and told the two women that they should feel really [5]_____ of their achievements.

6 Complete the sentences with the phrases below.

| get the verdict   making their decision |
| ~~puts the finishing touches~~   the winner is |

1 Becky *puts the finishing touches* to her model.

2 It's time to _____.

3 The judges are _____.

4 And _____ is Becky Hunt

7 Read the video script. Underline any words or phrases you don't know and find their meaning in your dictionary.

Part 1: The contest

The show that celebrates the very best of young hard-working British talent is back! These local heroes don't sing and dance. They just work very hard! They're all perfectionists in their work. And now for the second year running, they're going head to head.

5 They all want to prove that they're number one in their professions. From butchers to hairdressers … from beauticians to fishmongers. And they all feel really confident that they can win this competition.

Judging them will be two top experts who will look for winners in each category and … tell the others how badly they are doing.

10 There is no time for the contestants to be worried. They need to take a deep breath and just focus on what they are doing.

Part 2: The contestants

Tonight it's the turn of the hairdressers. They'll be designing different hairstyles that the judges request.

15 They'll be getting creative with different techniques. Can they handle the interview from hell? Can they design a truly original style? And in their toughest challenge, can they create a whole new head-to-toe look from nothing? That is not an easy thing to do. One of them will claim the title they all desire … the Young Hairdresser of the Year!

Let's meet the hairdressers. Finalist Number 1 from Birmingham is twenty-four-year-old

20 Lisa Farrell. She really wants to win this competition. She says that she's just going to go in there and just do what she does best, which is hair! Our second finalist is Serafina Woodward. She's twenty-two and from Hemel Hempstead. She is extremely passionate about hairdressing. This is her life. Doing hairdressing is how she can be creative. Finalist number three is from Southampton, twenty-four-year-old Becky Hunt.

25 This is what she's been working towards. Hopefully, she'll be able to stand out and show off a bit. And our fourth finalist from London representing the boys is twenty-year-old Jake Unger. For him, hairdressing is like a massive passion. It's like his first big love.

Part 3: The winner

Now it is just a contest between Becky and Serafina. Here, they are putting the finishing touches to their hairstyles. Serafina's style is very rock-and-roll, while Becky's look is much more alternative. Which one will convince the judges? Which one is the winning look?

Now they have to wait for the final result. Five, four, three, two, one. That's it. Time's up. It's the moment of truth. Both women have created their own distinct hairstyles. But this challenge is about the entire look: how well the clothes, shoes, make-up and hair come together.

It's time to push back the screen and see what our two finalists have created. The judges are very proud of both Becky and Serafina. It's been a really hard close decision but only one of them can win the title. And the Young Hairdresser of the Year … is Becky. Becky performed well during the whole competition and in the final challenge, she won with a completely original avant-garde look.

How does it feel to be Young Hairdresser of the Year? She can hardly believe it. What a couple of days it's been! Congratulations to Becky! Hard luck to Serafina. Our Young Hairdresser of the Year is Becky Hunt.

5

Light years away

VOCABULARY
Space | Dimensions and distance |
Large numbers | Space science

GRAMMAR
Zero, First and Second Conditionals |
Third Conditional

READING
Reading for specific detail

LISTENING
Taking notes

SPEAKING
Warnings and prohibition

WRITING
An essay

BBC CULTURE
Can you do sport in space?

I can talk about space and use large numbers.

1 ● Look at the pictures and complete the words related to space.

1 c <u>o m e t</u>

2 a _ _ _ _ _ _ _ _

3 International
S _ _ _ _ S _ _ _ _ _ _

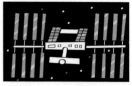

4 s _ _ _

5 p _ _ _ _ _ _

6 E _ _ _ _ _

7 o _ _ _ _

8 m _ _ _

2 ●● Write the correct word for each definition.

1 a scientist who studies the stars and planets **a**_stronomer_

2 a device which uses mirrors to make distant objects look larger and closer **t**_____

3 a vehicle that is able to travel in space **s**_____

4 a man-made object moving around a planet in space – it can send digital information across the world **s**_____

5 a person who travels in space **a**_____

6 a building with lights on the ceiling which show the movement of planets and stars **p**_____

7 the collection of eight planets (including Earth) and their moons that travel around the Sun **s**_____ **s**_____

8 a system of millions or billions of stars – ours is called the Milky Way **g**_____

3 ● **WORD FRIENDS** Decide if the pairs of sentences are the same (S) or different (D).

1 [S] The box is 120 centimetres long.
   The length is 120 centimetres.

2 [ ] We're ten kilometres away from home.
   We're travelling at ten kilometres an hour.

3 [ ] The mountain is 3,000 metres high.
   The width of the mountain is 3,000 metres.

4 [ ] I live five kilometres from school.
   My school is five kilometres away.

5 [ ] The speed limit is thirty kilometres per hour.
   The speed limit is thirty kilometres an hour.

4 ●● **WORD FRIENDS** Complete the sentences with one word in each gap.

1 The satellite is ten metres *long*.
2 The _____ is ten metres.
3 It's four metres _____.
4 The _____ is four metres.

5 Slow down! You're doing 120 kilometres per _____!

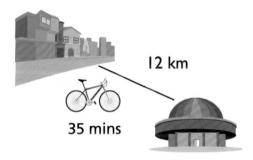

12 km

35 mins

6 I live twelve kilometres _____ the planetarium.
7 It usually _____ me thirty-five minutes to cycle there.

5 ● Write the numbers.

1 six hundred and fifty-eight ___*658*___
2 eight million three hundred thousand _____
3 three thousand seven hundred and sixty-nine _____
4 four billion eight hundred and seventy-two thousand _____
5 twenty-nine million six hundred and seventy-four thousand three hundred and fifty-two _____
6 nine point three million _____

6 ●● Write the numbers as words.

1 6,499   *six thousand four hundred and ninety-nine*
2 6.8 billion _____
3 7,000,300,000 _____
4 123 _____
5 476,000 _____
6 12,413,389,672 _____

7 ●● Choose the correct option.

1 The number of (satellites) / telescopes in the Earth's orbit at the moment is estimated to be two thousand two hundred and *seventy one / seventy-one*.
2 Our *galaxy / moon* is over a *hundred, thousand / hundred thousand* light years across.
3 The rocket is twenty metres *long / length* and it's *wide / width* is five metres.
4 The closest *star / spacecraft* to our sun is *four point two / four stop two* light years away.
5 This new rocket is a *spacecraft / planetarium* which can carry fifteen *astronomers / astronauts*.
6 I live ten kilometres *from / away* my school. It *takes / drives* twenty minutes to get there.
7 There are eight *planets / stars* in our *space station / solar system*.
8 If you look carefully through the *satellite / telescope*, you can sometimes see a *comet / moon*.

8 ●●● Complete the text with one word in each gap.

● ● ●

Space facts you might not know

The closest [1]*planet* to Earth is Venus, which is over forty billion kilometres [2]_____. The furthest planet from Earth in our solar [3]_____ is Neptune, which is up to 4.6 billion kilometres [4]_____ Earth. Some think that Pluto is the furthest at 7.47 billion kilometres away, but in 2006 scientists decided that Pluto is not actually a planet. The largest planet is Jupiter and it has at least sixty-seven [5]_____ in its orbit.

The first [6]_____ was Yuri Gagarin. He travelled on the [7]_____ Vostok 1 and in 1961 became the first man in space. Vostok 1 had a small width – only 2.3 metres [8]_____ and the mission lasted a hundred [9]_____ eight minutes. This was incredible at the time because a spacecraft has to travel at over 40,000 kilometres [10]_____ hour to leave the Earth's atmosphere.

I can talk about things that are always true, possible situations and imaginary situations.

1 ● **Choose the correct option.**

1 If the rocket (*launches*) / *launched* at the right time, it will reach the moon in six weeks.
2 You won't see the comet *unless* / *if* you have a good telescope.
3 I always watch *Star Watch* if *it's* / *it will be* on TV.
4 I wouldn't go into space if you *pay* / *paid* me!
5 Would you study astronomy if you *have* / *had* the chance?
6 If the weather isn't good, you *won't see* / *will see* the planet clearly.

2 ● **Order the words in brackets to complete the sentences.**

1 If you want to be an astronomer, *you need to study Physics* (Physics / need / study / to / you).
2 I'd come to the party _____
_____ (an exam / if / tomorrow / have / I / didn't).
3 _____
(out / Kate / go / won't / unless) the weather improves.
4 _____
(with us / if / want / you / to / come), I'll give you a lift.
5 If students fail the exam, _____
_____ (again / can / it / take / they).
6 If you could go anywhere in the world, _____
_____ (go / you / where / would)?

3 ●● **Complete the interview with an astronaut with the correct form of the verbs in brackets.**

Interviewer: Good afternoon, Colin. How are the preparations for the next mission going?
Astronaut: Very well, thanks. If the weather [1]*is* (be) good, we'll leave Earth on Friday, then if everything goes well, we [2]_____ (reach) the space station in two days.
Interviewer: Could anything go wrong?
Astronaut: Of course. For example, the weather might be bad. If that happened, we [3]_____ (wait) until it got better. Also, if any of the rocket's systems [4]_____ (fail), we would use the emergency spacecraft to return to Earth.
Interviewer: Well, let's hope everything goes well. What do people need to do if they [5]_____ (want) to see the space station from Earth?
Astronaut: Well, you [6]_____ (not see) the space station unless you have a good telescope. If you want to know when it passes over your area, [7]_____ (check) on our website.
Interviewer: Thanks very much, Colin, and good luck!

4 ●● **Use the prompts to write conditional sentences. Use the words in brackets.**

1 If / I / have / enough money / I / buy / telescope (would)
If I had enough money, I'd buy a telescope.
2 if / rain / weekend / we / visit / planetarium (we'll)
_____
3 I / travel / more / if / have / more time (had)
_____
4 if / the computer / get / too hot / switch / it / off (gets)
_____
5 my parents / not happy / if / I / not pass / my exams (won't)
_____

5 ●●● **Complete the text with the correct form of the verbs in brackets.**

Build your own telescope

If you [1]*want* (want) to see the stars and planets, you [2]_____ (can) make your own telescope. All you need is a cardboard tube – the ones you [3]_____ (use) if you want to send a poster by mail – and a couple of lenses. Make sure you cut the tube very straight. This is important, as you [4]_____ (not be able to) change the focus unless it [5]_____ (be) absolutely straight. Then attach the lenses inside the tube. You can just slide them in, but if you [6]_____ (need) to make them secure, glue them in carefully. Finally, cover the other end of the tube with card and make a small hole in the end to look through. Now you're ready to look at the stars! It's not the world's most powerful telescope, but if you [7]_____ (use) it on a clear night, you get some good views. If I [8]_____ (not have) mine, I wouldn't see so much of the night sky.

I can understand specific detail in an article.

1 Match words/phrases 1–8 with definitions a–h.

1 [b] attend
2 ☐ space camp
3 ☐ pilot's licence
4 ☐ training programme
5 ☐ 20/20 vision
6 ☐ weightless
7 ☐ mission
8 ☐ simulate

a the ability to see clearly, without glasses
b be present at (an event)
c an important job that involves travelling somewhere
d the qualification you need to fly a plane
e replicate the appearance or character of something
f a course of studying practical skills
g having little weight because there is no gravity, e.g. in space or under water
h a place where you stay in the summer and learn about space

2 Read the article. Put the topics a–f in the order they are mentioned.

a ☐ professional requirements
b ☐ how difficult it is
c ☐ work on the ground
d ☐ training
e ☐ physical requirements
f ☐ academic requirements

3 Read the article again. Choose the correct answers.

1 Which of the following do you need to become an astronaut?
   a academic qualifications
   b physical requirements
   c work experience
   d all three of the above

2 What's the minimum academic requirement to become an astronaut?
   a a PhD
   b a university degree
   c a school diploma
   d a pilot's licence

3 Why is it important to be very healthy?
   a Because it would be a big problem if you got ill in space.
   b So you can cope with the training.
   c Because you have to be strong to fly a spacecraft.
   d So you weigh less on the spacecraft.

4 What happens after you graduate as an astronaut candidate?
   a You go straight on to a space mission.
   b You do several years' more training.
   c You do several weeks' more training.
   d You take an exam.

So you want to be an astronaut?

Becoming an astronaut isn't easy. If you want to go into space one day, you'll have to spend many years training, studying and becoming physically fit and that's just the beginning. Only a small number of people who apply will successfully become astronauts.

The first step is getting a university qualification. NASA requires at least a first degree in Engineering, Science or Maths. But if you really want to succeed, you'll get a Master's or even a PhD. Attending space camp when you're a teenager helps too.

That's only the start. There are other requirements. You also need at least three years' professional experience in something similar (e.g. flying a plane with a pilot's licence). Alternatively, NASA also look for people who have worked as teachers.

You also need to be physically fit, with 20/20 vision, normal blood pressure and be between 157 and 190.5 cm tall. It's important that you're healthy, because if you became ill in space, it would be very expensive to bring you home for a medical emergency.

If you are selected, you'll begin a two-year training programme as an 'astronaut candidate'. You spend your time scuba diving, learning Russian, training in a weightless environment and many other things. Part of this training involves going up in the 'vomit comet', a special aeroplane which flies up and down to simulate weightlessness (and often makes people sick!).

If there are no problems, it will be many years before you are chosen to go on a mission. During this time, you'll do more training and work on the ground, helping with missions already out in space. Becoming an astronaut takes a lot of hard work, patience and determination, but if you're lucky, you'll become one of the few people to see Earth from space!

I can talk about unreal situations in the past.

1 ● Complete the sentences with the words below. There is one extra word.

| had   hadn't   ~~have~~   if
| launched   would   wouldn't

1 If I hadn't studied engineering, I wouldn't _have_ become interested in space travel.

2 We wouldn't have reached the moon late if we'd _____ the rocket on time.

3 _____ the captain hadn't been ill, he wouldn't have left the mission.

4 What would you have done if you _____ passed the physical exam?

5 I _____ have become an astronaut if I hadn't learnt to fly a plane.

6 If they had launched the rocket two seconds earlier, it _____ have crashed.

2 ● Choose the correct option.

What would have happened?

Have you ever had any moments where something bad happened, but something good came out of it? Tell us about it below.

Last year my long-term girlfriend broke up with me. It was terrible, but if I'd stayed with her, I [1]would / _wouldn't_ have met Kate. She's been my girlfriend for three months now and she's great!

Yesterday I woke up late and missed the bus for school, so I had to take my bicycle. But I would have been even later if I [2]took / 'd taken the bus, because there was a terrible traffic jam!

For our Science project last month, my teacher made me work with someone I didn't like. But if she hadn't made us work together, we [3]wouldn't have / wouldn't become friends.

Last week I was at a party when my dad arrived to pick me up – so embarrassing! But when we got home, I realised that the last bus had left before he arrived, so I would have been stuck if he [4]hadn't arrived / arrived!

A few months ago my mum made me clean out the garage. It took me ages and I didn't enjoy the work, but I wouldn't have [5]found / find my dad's old book on astronomy if I hadn't cleaned the garage. Now I'm really interested in it!

3 ●● Match 1–5 with a–e to make sentences. Then complete the sentences with the correct form of the verbs in brackets.

1 [d] I would have come and found you

2 ☐ If Ollie had saved more money,

3 ☐ They wouldn't have bought a telescope

4 ☐ If I'd been with you,

5 ☐ If we'd known it was going to be so cold,

a I _____ (not let) you buy that expensive jacket.

b we _____ (wear) warmer clothes.

c he _____ (be able to) buy those trainers.

d if I _'d known_ (know) you were at the party.

e if it _____ (not be) so cheap.

4 ●●● Read the text. Choose the correct answers.

An amazing rescue

On 11 April 1970 Apollo 13 flew into space from Florida, USA. If the mission [1]___ successful, Apollo 13 would have been the third manned spacecraft to land on the moon. However, after two days, there was an explosion. If an oxygen tank [2]___ exploded, the spacecraft would [3]___ landed on the moon. But instead, the mission stopped and the spacecraft orbited the moon instead. The flight director, Gene Kranz, wanted to use the moon's gravity to push the spacecraft back to Earth. If he hadn't [4]___ this decision, the astronauts [5]___ survived. One of the biggest problems of the return journey was removing carbon dioxide from the spacecraft. If engineers on Earth [6]___ invented a system to do this quickly, the astronauts wouldn't have [7]___ able to breathe. Finally, on 17 April, the astronauts returned safely to Earth.

1 a	was	b	were	(c)	had been
2 a	hadn't	b	wouldn't	c	would
3 a	had	b	haven't	c	have
4 a	make	b	made	c	making
5 a	wouldn't have	b	would have	c	hadn't had
6 a	hadn't	b	had	c	wouldn't
7 a	had	b	been	c	be

I can understand the main points of a report about space science.

1 Complete the puzzle. What is the mystery word?

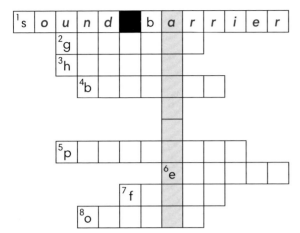

¹s	o	u	n	d		b	a	r	r	i	e	r
			²g									
			³h									
			⁴b									
⁵p												
					⁶e							
			⁷f									
⁸o												

1 the sudden increased pressure against a vehicle when it travels at near the speed of sound
2 the force that causes something to fall to the ground
3 a gas which is lighter than air
4 a large bag filled with gas so that it rises in the air
5 a large piece of material that fills with air and helps the wearer fall slowly to the ground
6 a machine which produces power to make a vehicle move
7 physical power which moves something
8 we need this gas to breathe

2 Complete the sentences with words from Exercise 1.

1 After jumping from the plane, Sam opened his *parachute* and fell safely to the ground.
2 There is less _____ on the moon than on Earth, so you can jump really high.
3 For my mum's birthday, my dad took her on a hot-air _____ ride, high across the countryside.
4 Plants take in carbon dioxide and release _____.
5 The car has a very powerful _____ and can go from 0 to 100 kilometres per hour in nine seconds.
6 The satellite exploded when re-entering the Earth's _____.
7 If you travel faster than 1234 kilometres per hour, you break the _____.

3 🔊 10 Listen to the first part of a podcast about space debris and choose the correct answer.

What is space debris?
a a type of satellite
b what's left when something large is destroyed in an explosion or fire
c everything that's in orbit around the Earth

4 🔊 11 Listen to the rest of the podcast. Which two topics are NOT mentioned?

1 ☐ the number of small pieces of debris
2 ☐ the problems of large debris
3 ☐ missions to other planets
4 ☐ the most dangerous area
5 ☐ broken spacecraft
6 ☐ Earth's orbit around the sun
7 ☐ cleaning up the debris

5 🔊 11 Listen again. Complete the notes with one word or number in each gap.

Space debris

● More than ¹_____ million debris smaller than 1 cm.
● Just one piece of debris can damage a spacecraft or ²_____.
● International Space Station (ISS) uses Whipple Shields to make debris ³_____.
● Nearly 30,000 pieces larger than ⁴_____ cm.
● One piece has landed every day on Earth for last ⁵_____ years.
● We don't clean it up because it's too ⁶_____.

I can give a warning and tell somebody not to do something.

1 Choose the correct option.

1 Look *careful* / (*out*)! You nearly walked into me!

2 *Make* / *Do* sure you don't leave the door open.

3 You aren't *careful* / *allowed* to leave your bikes here.

4 *Mind* / *Be* careful – this plate is very hot.

5 *Mind* / *Look* the floor – it's wet.

6 Keep *off* / *away* the grass – you must stay on the paths.

2 Complete the sentences with the words below.

| careful   do   ~~don't~~   for |
| mustn't   out |

1 *Don't* fly your drone here.

2 Mind _____! You nearly flew it into that man.

3 You _____ fly your drone over private property.

4 If you're not _____, it'll go up too fast and then fall to the ground.

5 You can't _____ that – it's really dangerous.

6 Watch out _____ those birds.

3 Write the phrases from Exercises 1 and 2 in the correct column.

Warning	Prohibition
Look out!	_____
_____	_____
_____	_____
_____	_____
_____	

4 Match 1–3 with a–c to make sentences. **OUT** of class

1 ☐ We're

2 ☐ Can I

3 ☐ That's so

a have a go?   b neat!   c off!

5 Complete the dialogues with the phrases from Exercise 4.

1 A: OK, ready?

   B: Ready. And _____! Oh my days, look at it fly!

2 A: What are you studying?

   B: Space science.

   A: Really? _____!

3 A: Is that your drone?

   B: Yes.

   A: I've never flown one before. _____?

6 🔊 12 Complete the dialogues with one word in each gap. Listen and check.

Seb: Look at me!

Mother: Watch [1]*out*! If you're not [2]_____, you'll fall.

Jason: Look [3]_____! Here comes the park ranger.

Harry: What's the problem?

Ranger: You aren't [4]_____ to play football here. See that sign there?

Harry: Oh yeah, it says '[5]_____ off the grass.' Sorry.

Man: Mind [6]_____! You nearly walked in front of that car!

Woman: Oh my days! Thanks!

Man: You really [7]_____ text when you're crossing the road.

Ivor: I'm going for a swim in the lake.

Becky: You can't do [8]_____! It's dangerous.

Ivor: No, it isn't. It's completely safe. See? There are some people swimming over there.

Becky: Oh, OK then, but [9]_____ careful. [10]_____ out for crocodiles.

Ivor: Don't worry. Wait. What did you say?!

I can write an essay discussing advantages and disadvantages.

1 Read the essay quickly and choose the best title.

   a   Should we send people to Mars?

   b   Is space exploration a good thing?

   c   Which planet should we visit next?

[1]*Many people believe* that the next step in space exploration is sending astronauts to Mars. It sounds exiting, but [2]_____ it?

[3]_____, we might discover things we need on Earth – like oil or gas. [4]_____ , we already know that there is a lot of the gas methane on Mars and it can be used to make plastic. [5]_____ we could discover new forms of life. [6]_____ there is frozen water on Mars and possibly even running water. This may mean there are other forms of life there.

[7]_____, a manned mission to Mars would be incredibly expensive, at over $50 billion. The spacecraft would need to take food, water, oxygen and medical supplies and these things would have to be launched into space. [8]_____ we could spend this money on solving the problems we already have on Earth. [9]_____, it's very dangerous. We don't know the effects of being in space and of weightlessness on the human body for such a long period of time. In [10]_____ the possible human cost is too great a risk.

[11]_____, while living on Mars might seem like a good idea, I think we have big problems to solve on Earth first.

2 Complete gaps 1–6 in the essay with phrases a–f.

   a   For example

   b   Many people believe

   c   It seems

   d   On the one hand

   e   Another advantage is that

   f   is it worth

3 Complete gaps 7–11 in the essay with phrases a–e.

   a   my opinion

   b   To sum up,

   c   I believe

   d   On the other hand,

   e   Moreover,

4 Match the paragraphs with the parts of the essay.

> advantages   conclusion   disadvantages   introduction

Paragraph 1: _____   Paragraph 3: _____

Paragraph 2: _____   Paragraph 4: _____

5 Choose the correct option.

   1   To sum *off* / *up*, I believe space exploration is a good idea.

   2   One reason *to* / *for* doing this is to find another planet to live on.

   3   Nowadays, *more and more* / *more and most* people believe we should travel in space.

   4   The *most* / *main* disadvantage is a lack of technology.

   5   *In* / *From* my opinion, we have more important problems here on Earth.

   6   *On other hand* / *Finally*, it could be a stepping stone for further space exploration.

6 Match sentences 1–6 from Exercise 5 with the headings.

Introduction: *3*

Arguments for/against: _____ , _____ , _____

Giving opinions: _____

Ending your essay: _____

7 Complete the notes with the words and phrases below.

> dangerous   expensive   new types   population problems   ~~to save~~

Should we spend money on finding another planet to live on?

For:
- might not be able [1]**to save** this planet
- discover [2]_____ of life
- growing [3]_____ on Earth and limited space

Against:
- too [4]_____ – billions of dollars
- [5]_____ on Earth more urgent
- too [6]_____ – could die in space

8 Look at the notes in Exercise 7. Write an essay answering the essay question. Follow the instructions below.

   1   Use the essay in Exercise 1 as a model.

   2   Include the following in your essay:

      •   an introduction and conclusion

      •   the advantages and disadvantages

      •   reasons for your opinions.

   3   Use phrases from Exercises 2, 3 and 5.

For each learning objective, tick (✓) the box that best matches your ability.

☺☺ = I understand and can help a friend.

☺ = I understand and can do it by myself.

☹ = I understand but have some questions.

☹☹ = I do not understand.

		☺☺	☺	☹	☹☹	Need help?	Now try ...
5.1	Vocabulary					Students' Book pp. 58–59 Workbook pp. 54–55	Ex. 1–2, p. 63
5.2	Grammar					Students' Book p. 60 Workbook p. 56	Ex. 3–4, p. 63
5.3	Reading					Students' Book p. 61 Workbook p. 57	
5.4	Grammar					Students' Book p. 62 Workbook p. 58	Ex. 4–5, p. 63
5.5	Listening					Students' Book p. 63 Workbook p. 59	
5.6	Speaking					Students' Book p. 64 Workbook p. 60	Ex. 6, p. 63
5.7	Writing					Students' Book p. 65 Workbook p. 61	

5.1   I can talk about space and use large numbers.

5.2   I can talk about things that are always true, possible situations and imaginary situations.

5.3   I can understand specific detail in an article.

5.4   I can talk about unreal situations in the past.

5.5   I can understand the main points of a report about space science.

5.6   I can give a warning and tell somebody not to do something.

5.7   I can write an essay discussing advantages and disadvantages.

What can you remember from this unit?

New words I learned (the words you most want to remember from this unit)	**Expressions and phrases I liked** (any expressions or phrases you think sound nice, useful or funny)	**English I heard or read outside class** (e.g. from websites, books, adverts, films, music)

Vocabulary

1 Complete the sentences with the nouns below. There is one extra noun.

> atmosphere   engine   galaxy   gravity
> orbit   satellite   solar system

1   The jet _____ in the spacecraft makes it fly very fast.
2   The recent mission sent a _____ into space to improve communication systems.
3   There are billions of stars in our _____ .
4   The Earth takes one year to _____ the sun.
5   The Earth's _____ protects us from the sun's rays and allows us to breathe.
6   _____ makes things fall to the ground.

2 Complete the words for each definition.

1   the word for 1,000,000   **m** _ _ _ _ _ _
2   someone who studies the stars
    a _ _ _ _ _ _ _ _ _
3   an icy rock travelling through space with a 'tail' of gas   **c** _ _ _ _ _
4   ours has eight planets in it   **s** _ _ _ _ _
    s _ _ _ _ _
5   the measurement of how wide something is
    w _ _ _ _ _
6   something you use to look at the stars
    t _ _ _ _ _ _ _ _ _
7   the measurement of how high something is
    h _ _ _ _ _ _
8   the Earth is one of these   **p** _ _ _ _ _ _

Grammar

3 Choose the correct option. Then mark each sentence 0 (Zero Conditional), 1 (First Conditional), 2 (Second Conditional) or 3 (Third Conditional).

1   If we *have / had* more money, we'd go to space camp.   ___
2   If I'm not too tired after school, I usually *go / went* cycling in the park.   ___
3   I wouldn't *meet / have met* Alice if I hadn't gone to the party.   ___
4   Tina *won't come / will come* to the picnic unless the weather is good.   ___
5   You look ill. I wouldn't go out today if I *am / were* you.   ___
6   If my team *would win / wins* the championship, I'll dance in the street!   ___

4 Complete the text with the correct form of the verbs in brackets.

> When I'm older, I want to be an astronaut. I'm sure if I work really hard, I [1]_____ (achieve) my dream one day. It's all I think about at the moment! If I have any free time, I [2]_____ (study) Physics or read about space technology online. When people ask me, 'What would you do if you [3]_____ (win) the lottery?' the answer is easy: I [4]_____ (buy) a tourist ticket to travel to space! I know I [5]_____ (not have) a chance unless I'm physically fit too. So if the weather's good at weekends I [6]_____ (play) sport or [7]_____ (go) running. What about you? If you could do any job at all, what [8]_____ (you/do)?

5 Complete the Third Conditional sentences about a school play that went wrong.

1	If I _____ (remember) my lines, the audience _____ (not laugh) at me.
2	People _____ (stay) until the end if the play _____ (not be) so boring.
3	The director _____ (not be) so angry if Ella _____ (wear) the right costume.
4	It _____ (be) better if Dave _____ (not fall) off the stage!
5	If everyone _____ (turn off) their mobile phones, they _____ (not ring) during the play!

Speaking language practice

6 Choose the correct option.

1   You aren't *can / allowed / have* to fly drones near an airport.
2   *Watch / Be / Get* out for people trying to steal your bag.
3   Look *in / on / out*! You nearly walked straight into me!
4   *Make / Do / Mind* sure you don't park in that road after 9 a.m.
5   Keep *out / in / off* the grass in this park.
6   If you're not *sure / careful / out*, you'll hurt yourself.

1 Match the sports below with the pictures. There are two extra words.

> baseball BMXing frisbee ~~golf~~ parkour
> skateboarding skydiving zorbing

1 *golf*   2 _____   3 _____

4 _____   5 _____   6 _____

2 Match the nouns below with definitions 1–6.

> crew gravity ~~harness~~ lab obstacle course
> surroundings

1 ropes or ties to keep someone or
   something in place   *harness*
2 a place where scientists do
   experiments   _____
3 people who work on a plane,
   spacecraft, etc.   _____
4 the things which are around you   _____
5 the force on Earth that holds us to
   the ground   _____
6 a number of objects you run or
   jump over   _____

3 Choose the correct option.

1 If you want to do sport in space, you have to
   (adapt)/ *tie* to your surroundings.
2 He ran the race to *run / raise* money for charity.
3 The International Space Station *travels /
   orbits* the Earth every ninety minutes.
4 Astronauts *do / have* sport in space to keep
   fit and active.
5 Have you ever *taken part / jumped out* in
   a marathon?
6 When you *return / throw* a boomerang in the
   space station, it comes back to you!

4 Complete the sentences with the correct form of the verbs below. There is one extra verb.

> crash encourage ~~grow~~ parachute perform

1 George Moyes says he doesn't want to *grow*
   old gracefully.
2 After jumping out of the plane, George
   _____ down onto Salisbury plain.
3 Aaron was the first person to _____
   a backflip in a wheelchair.
4 His brother _____ him a lot when he
   was child.

5 Use the prompts to write sentences about Aaron and George.

1 George's family / feel / worried / about his
   skydiving
   George's family felt worried about his skydiving.

2 George / not be / a typical ninety-seven-
   year-old
   _____

3 when / Aaron / be / eight, / he / start /
   wheelchair motocross
   _____

4 today / Aaron / travel / around the world /
   do / tricks and stunts
   _____

6 Read the video script. Underline any words or phrases you don't know and find their meaning in your dictionary.

Part 1: George Moyes – skydiver

Narrator:	With his tweed jacket and silk tie, George Moyes is not your typical skydiver. But then George Moyes, a retired shop window dresser, is not your typical ninety-seven-year-old. This was to be his first ever jump. His family – terrified. The man himself – ice cool.
Interviewer:	There'll be people watching this, thinking… 'What on earth is he doing? Why is it important for you to do it?'
George:	I'm saying the same thing myself, actually.
Narrator:	Ten minutes and 10,000 feet later, it's time to go. Free-falling at 120 miles an hour, then gently parachuting back down onto Salisbury plain.
Interviewer:	How was that?
George:	Lovely.
Interviewer:	Lovely?
George:	Yeah.
Trainer:	You can see he's pretty bonkers. He doesn't want to grow old gracefully. He's still got his own eyes, own ears. OK, he's got false teeth but apart from that, he's 100 percent there.
Interviewer:	Would you do it again?
George:	Yeah.
Interviewer:	Really?
George:	Oh, yeah.
Interviewer:	On his 100th birthday … a couple of years to go.
George:	That's right, yeah.

Part 2: Aaron Fotheringham – extreme wheelchair athlete

Narrator:	Aaron Fotheringham, known as 'Wheelz', is an extreme wheelchair athlete. Think about it: If you were in wheelchair, would you try this?
Aaron:	I ride WCMX. I'm from Las Vegas, Nevada. WCMX stands for *wheelchair motocross*. It's kind of like BMX but with wheelchairs, in skate parks and on ramps and stuff. I started riding WCMX when I was eight years old. My older brother was a BMXer and he always did skating too and just, you know, got me into it. I crashed a couple of times and he helped get me back up. And then I finally rolled away from one of them and I was like, 'That was fun!' You know, just instantly hooked on it. About six months after my first backflip, I ended up going to Germany and travelling for my first time because of the sport. And then from there it just hasn't let up.
Narrator:	This is the Venice Beach skate park and we're at an event called Life Rolls On. The best riders in the world come here. People of all ages are here, too. This is a young girl who wants to do a hand plant and a backflip. Aaron is a great teacher; he encourages everybody and shows them the skills they need.
Aaron:	Mainly, for me it's just important that they see the wheelchair as an, you know, opportunity, something fun. Because a lot of people think of the wheelchair as a dead-end. But you know, these kids, you know, you ask any of them, and they love their wheelchair! That's my goal.
Narrator:	Aaron is an example to everyone. He was the first person to perform a backflip in a wheelchair at the age of fourteen and he's always trying to do new tricks and stunts. He still gets nervous before the big jumps but he says that's part of the fun of it! If he didn't get nervous, he would stop.

6

Take a deep breath

I can talk about health problems.

1 ● **Match the words below with the descriptions.**

> asthma   food poisoning   hay fever   infection
> injury   insomnia   ~~migraine~~   travel sickness

1   My head hurts, I have a pain behind my eyes and I feel sick.   _migraine_
2   I cut my hand yesterday. Now it's red and feels hot.   _____
3   In the summer when I go outside, I have a runny nose and itchy eyes.   _____
4   Sometimes it's very difficult for me to breathe.   _____
5   I can't sleep at night.   _____
6   I feel sick on long car journeys.   _____
7   I ate some seafood earlier and now I'm feeling really sick.   _____
8   I've broken my arm.   _____

2 ●● **Complete the health problems in the comments**

1   Ouch! That looks like a nasty **i** _n j u r y_!

2   Don't give Tom any of those nuts – he has an **a** _ _ _ _ _ _ _.

3   I feel terrible – I think I've got a **v** _ _ _ _ _.

4   I love going for country walks, but my **h** _ _ **f** _ _ _ _ sometimes spoils it.

5   Make sure you wash that cut. You don't want to get an **i** _ _ _ _ _ _ _ _ _.

6   Our teacher isn't here today. She's at home with a stomach **b** _ _ _.

3 ● **WORD FRIENDS**   **Match verbs 1–6 with nouns a–f.**

1	_b_ get	a	your voice
2	☐ lose	b	lots of rest
3	☐ take	c	in bed
4	☐ have	d	your chest
5	☐ listen to	e	a nose bleed
6	☐ stay	f	your temperature

4 ●● [WORD FRIENDS] **Choose a verb from A and a noun from B to complete the sentences.**

A
come down   get   having   lost   ~~stay~~   take

B
appetite   ~~bed~~   check-up   flu   prescription   tablets

1 You must _stay_ in _bed_ until you feel better. Don't even try to get up.
2 I don't want anything to eat, thanks. I've _____ my _____ .
3 You need to _____ these _____ twice a day with food.
4 I need to see the doctor so I can _____ a _____ for my blood pressure medicine.
5 Sorry, I can't make it to the game today. I've _____ with the _____ .
6 I'm going to the doctor's today. Don't worry, nothing's wrong. I'm just _____ a _____ .

5 ● **Complete the dialogue with the words below.**

deep   hurt   ~~matter~~   serious   something
take   worry

Doctor: Good morning. What seems to be the ¹_matter_ ?
Alice: I'm in pain, doctor.
Doctor: I see. Where does it ²_____ ?
Alice: Just here – above my stomach.
Doctor: OK … let me see. Now, take a ³_____ breath.
Alice: Is it ⁴_____ ?
Doctor: Oh no. It's nothing to ⁵_____ about. It's just a stomach bug.
Alice: That's good. Is there anything I can ⁶_____ for it?
Doctor: Yes, here's ⁷_____ for the pain.

6 ●● **Complete the table.**

Noun	Verb	Adjective
asthma	–	_asthmatic_
	infect	
	–	ill
pain	–	
	prescribe	–

7 ●● **Complete the sentences with the correct adjective or noun form of the words below.**

asthma   ill   infect (x2)   pain   prescribe

1 The place where I cut myself is red and painful – I think the cut is _infected_ .
2 The doctor gave me a _____ for antibiotics.
3 Keep that cut covered up or you might get an _____ .
4 I can't move my leg – it's too _____ .
5 I have to use an inhaler because I'm _____ .
6 Tara missed a lot of school this year because of her _____ .

8 ●●● **Complete the text with one word in each gap.**

Nuts about nuts

On Saturday I woke up feeling really awful. I had ¹_lost_ my appetite and I felt sick. My mum ²_____ my temperature and saw I ³_____ a rash all over my face and neck. She thought it might be ⁴_____ poisoning, so she immediately took me to the doctor's. The doctor asked me, 'What's the ⁵_____ ?' and I showed her the rash. I also told her it's ⁶_____ when I swallow. In the end, she told me I have a food ⁷_____ – I'm ⁸_____ to nuts. She gave me a(n) ⁹_____ to take to the chemist's and told me to stay in ¹⁰_____ until I felt better.

I can report what somebody else has said.

1 ● Match direct statements and questions 1–6 with reported speech a–f.

1 [d] 'I'm having a check-up.'
2 [ ] 'Are you having a check-up?'
3 [ ] 'I'll have a check-up.'
4 [ ] 'I had a check-up.'
5 [ ] 'What time is your check-up?'
6 [ ] 'You can have a check-up.'

a She told me she would have a check-up.
b She said I could have a check-up.
c She asked me what time my check-up was.
d She said she was having a check-up.
e She asked me if I was having a check-up.
f She said she'd had a check-up.

2 ●● Choose the correct option.

1 My dad asked me what time *was my appointment* / (*my appointment was*).
2 She said she had seen the doctor *the day before* / *yesterday*.
3 The doctor said he *will* / *would* take my blood pressure.
4 Charles asked us *if we were* / *were we* going on holiday this year.
5 After the injury, Linda said she *can't* / *couldn't* feel her arm.

3 ●● Order the words to make reported statements and questions.

1 they / me / how often / the medicine / took / asked / I
   They asked me how often I took the medicine.
2 James / wanted / if / I / asked / to go / me / for pizza
   _____
3 me / told / Julia / was feeling / she / bad
   _____
4 if / Carl / the doctor / asked / help / would / the medicine
   _____

5 the book / her / I / was enjoying / told / I
   _____
6 before / told / David / been / us / had / he / there
   _____

4 ●● Rewrite the statements and questions in reported speech.

Who do you think will win the race?

1 She asked us *who we thought would win the race*.

I want to be a scientist.

2 He said _____.

I went to the doctor yesterday.

3 She said _____.

What can we do to help Gary pass his exams?

4 He asked us _____.

I'm having a party this weekend.

5 She told us _____.

Do you study Biology at school?

6 He asked me _____.

5 ●●● Read the text. Choose the correct answers.

The other day my sister Charis and her husband told me some excellent news. They said they ^{1}___ a baby, and that I ^{2}___ an uncle! They said they ^{3}___ the week before, but wanted to be sure everything was OK before they told me. The doctor said he ^{4}___ worried at first because my sister ^{5}___ ill recently, but he checked carefully and the baby is healthy. They asked me ^{6}___ any ideas about her name. I told them I ^{7}___ to call her Carla because my name's Carl. Unfortunately, they said they ^{8}___ that idea!

1 a had   b had had   (c) were having
2 a are soon   b would soon be   c was soon
3 a would find out b had found out   c were finding out
4 a had been   b will be   c would be
5 a is   b will be   c had been
6 a if I was having b if I had   c have I had
7 a had wanted   b wanted   c would want
8 a didn't like   b weren't liking   c hadn't liked

I can find specific detail in different types of text.

1 Match the words below with the definitions.

| bandage   burn   concussion
| ~~myth~~   symptom   throat

1 something which isn't true *myth*
2 the area at the back of your mouth
   _____
3 a head injury that makes you feel ill or become unconscious
   _____
4 a long thin piece of material that you put around a cut _____
5 an injury you get from touching something very hot _____
6 one of the effects of an illness
   _____

2 Read the article. Match pictures A–E with 'myths' 1–5.

3 Read the article again. Mark the sentences T (true) or F (false).

1 ☐ If you have a nosebleed, you should make yourself sick to get the blood out of your throat.
2 ☐ You shouldn't do anything after swallowing poison until you've spoken to a doctor.
3 ☐ You should put hot water on a burn.
4 ☐ The man in the TV programme fell asleep and didn't wake up again.
5 ☐ It's not cold weather that causes the flu, but it can make it worse.

4 Answer the questions. Use no more than three words.

1 After putting your head down, what should you do to stop a nosebleed?
2 What might poison do if you make yourself sick?
3 What might you get if you put butter on a burn?
4 What must you be able to do for it to be OK to sleep with concussion?
5 What causes the flu?

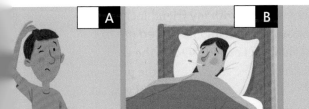

Five common myths about illness and injury

1 Put your head back if you have a nosebleed.

The myth: In the past, people said that you had to put your head back to stop the blood.
Why it's wrong: The blood can go down your throat and you might be sick.
What you should do: Sit down, put your head down and hold your nose. In about ten minutes the nosebleed will stop.

2 If you drink poison, make yourself sick to get it out.

The myth: In the past, people thought that if you had swallowed poison by mistake, you had to be sick to get the poison out of your body.
Why it's wrong: It can do more damage when it comes back up, and it might burn your throat.

What you should do: Every poison is different, so contact a doctor immediately.

3 Put butter on a burn.

The myth: When I was little, my grandmother told me I had to put butter on my skin if I burnt it.
Why it's wrong: It can give you an infection and make the injury worse!
What you should do: Put the burn under cold water for a few minutes, then put a bandage on it to protect the burnt area and stop infection.

4 If someone has concussion, don't let them sleep.

The myth: I watched a TV programme recently where a man hit his head and his friend told him that he shouldn't fall asleep or he might not wake up again.
Why it's wrong: You might have concussion and one of the

symptoms is feeling tired. If you are awake and can speak and walk, rest is actually one of the best ways to treat concussion. But if you are worried you have a head injury, see your doctor.
What you should do: Get some rest!

5 Wear warm clothes in winter so that you don't come down with the flu.

The myth: Cold weather causes the flu.
Why it's wrong: It's a good idea to prepare for cold weather by wearing warm clothes, but the cold temperature doesn't cause the flu. The only thing that can cause the flu is the flu virus. If you already have this virus, then the flu symptoms can get worse.
What you should do: Eat healthily and do exercise to stay strong.

I can use reported speech to talk about commands and requests.

1 ● Complete the sentences with the words below.

| asked   me   not   to   ~~told~~   us

1 'Put it down.'
 She *told* me to put it down.
2 'Lie down, please.'
 The doctor _____ me to lie down.
3 'Everybody, listen carefully, please.'
 The teacher asked _____ to listen carefully.
4 'Don't work too hard.'
 He told us _____ to work too hard.
5 'Lift your arm, please.'
 The nurse asked _____ to lift my arm.
6 'Fill in the form.'
 The man told me _____ fill in the form.

2 ● Choose the correct option.

1

Dad: Hey! I asked you ¹*be / to be* quiet!
Molly: Sorry! It's just that Jane ²*asked me to / asked to* help her with her Music project.
Dad: OK, but turn the volume down. Mum's trying to sleep and she asked us ³*not to make / to not make* any noise.

2

Meg: Jamie, can you help me with my Maths homework? I ⁴*told / asked* Dad to help, but he's busy.
Jamie: Sure, what do you have to do?
Meg: The teacher told us ⁵*to do / do* the exercises on this page.

3 ●● Order the words in brackets to complete the sentences.

1 He asked *us to pay attention* (attention / us / pay / to).
2 The doctor _____ _____ (me / stay / to / told) in bed.
3 My sister asked _____ _____ (her / take / me / to) temperature.
4 I _____ _____ (be / you / told / to) quiet!
5 She told _____ _____ (her / not / me / read / to) diary.
6 I _____ _____ (to / asked / use / not / you) your mobile phone in class.

4 ●● Use the prompts to write reported commands and requests.

1 the teacher / ask / we / listen / carefully
 The teacher asked us to listen carefully.
2 Carole / tell / we / not leave / rubbish / in her car
 _____
3 I / ask / they / sit / over there
 _____
4 doctor / tell / me / not play / sport / for two weeks
 _____
5 Sarah / ask / James / meet / she / after school
 _____

5 ●●● Complete the text with reported commands and statements. Use the correct form of the prompts below.

| ~~ask / me / call~~   ask / me / describe   ask / me / phone
ask / me / tell   ask / they / let   tell / he / sit down
tell / me / make sure   tell / me / not panic

Last week, I was with my friend Joel when he said he was in pain and he ¹*asked me to call* an ambulance. I called 999 and the woman on the phone ² _____ the problem. She also ³ _____ her if Joel was taking any medicine. Then she ⁴ _____ he was comfortable, so I ⁵ _____ and not move. The woman on the phone said the ambulance would be there in a few minutes and ⁶ _____ , which was difficult! When the ambulance arrived, they took Joel to hospital and I ⁷ _____ me come too. When we got there, they told me he had appendicitis and ⁸ _____ his parents. In the end, he had an operation and was fine.

6 Choose the correct option. **O**UT of class

a Please *be / have* serious!
b I was just messing *over / about*.
c *What / Very* funny!

7 Complete the dialogues with phrases a–c from Exercise 6.

1 A: _____ We don't have much time left!
 B: Alright! I just wanted to have some fun.
2 A: Boo!
 B: Agh! _____ You made me jump!
3 A: I think you really upset Joanna.
 B: Really? _____

I can listen for specific detail and talk about extreme sports.

1 Look at the pictures and complete the words for extreme sports.

1 B*MXing*

2 s_____

3 h____-g_____

4 s_____

5 k____-s_____

6 c_____

7 f____r_____

8 b_____j_____

9 s____-d____

10 b_____

11 a_____

12 p_____

13 w____-w____
r_____

14 p_____

2 Complete what the people are saying. Use extreme sports from Exercise 1.

1 I tried <u>sandboarding</u> for the first time on holiday. We went down the dunes in the desert. It was really exciting!

2 _____ is scary at first, but as soon as you jump out of the plane, you forget to be afraid and just enjoy the view.

3 I've been into _____ since I was little. It's great fun to compete in races and it keeps you fit.

4 I could never do _____. I hate high places, so I find the idea of going down a rock with a rope terrifying.

5 _____ is great fun, but if it's not windy enough, then you get very wet when you fall into the sea!

6 I've done _____ once – from a really high bridge in South Africa. Amazing!

3 🔊 13 Listen to Keiran talking about an extreme sports camp. Put the sports a–e in the order he talks about them. There is one extra sport.

a ☐ abseiling
b ☐ bungee jumping
c ☐ parachute jump
d ☐ BMXing
e ☐ sandboarding

4 🔊 13 Listen again. Complete the notes with the missing information.

ESC

◉ ESC = Extreme Sports ¹_____

◉ How long: ²_____ weeks

◉ BMX: you'll learn how to go fast, plus impressive ³_____

◉ Abseiling: first practise on the indoor climbing ⁴_____

◉ Parachuting: ⁵_____ days training

◉ Check your health with a short ⁶_____

◉ Book by: ⁷_____ June

◉ Cost: £ ⁸_____ – includes food, ⁹_____ and equipment

6.6 SPEAKING   Asking for and giving advice

I can ask for and give advice.

1 Match 1–5 with a–e to make dialogues.

1 [d] I've got a sore throat. What's your advice?

2 ☐ I've got a nosebleed. Any ideas what to do?

3 ☐ Ugh! I feel sick. If you were me, what would you do?

4 ☐ I've got a weird rash on my arm. What do you suggest?

5 ☐ I've got a migraine. Any ideas what to do?

a If I were you, I'd stop playing on your computer.

b Try putting some cream on it.

c I'd recommend sitting down and holding your nose.

d Have you tried drinking some tea with honey and lemon?

e You should stop eating all those chocolates!

2 Order the words to make sentences.

1 suggest / do / what / you / ?
   What do you suggest?

2 go / if / you, / I'd / to the doctor / I / were
   _____

3 taking / have / tried / you / vitamin C / ?
   _____

4 to / any / what / do / ideas / ?
   _____

5 help / could / wish / I / I
   _____

6 afraid / you / I / can't / I'm / help / really
   _____

3 Complete the sentences with one word in each gap.

1 You *ought* to have a check-up.

2 If you were me, what _____ you do?

3 I wish I _____ suggest something, but I can't.

4 Have you thought _____ eating more healthily?

5 _____ is your advice?

6 I don't know what to suggest, I'm _____.

7 It _____ be a good idea to see a doctor.

8 You'd _____ go to bed until you feel better.

4 Order the words to make phrases. **OUT of class**

a sounds / I / it / weird / know
   _____

b a / I'll / go / give / it
   _____

c me / driving / it's / mad / !
   _____

5 Complete the dialogues with the phrases from Exercise 4.

1 A: I've got hiccups! Any ideas what to do?
   B: _____, but try holding your breath and counting to ten.

2 A: What's that noise?
   B: I don't know, but _____!

3 A: I feel tired all the time. What's your advice?
   B: If I were you, I'd eat more healthily.
   A: OK. _____.

6 🔊 14 Complete the dialogue with one word in each gap. Listen and check.

Jan: What's the matter, Liz? You look ill.

Liz: I keep getting these headaches. They get worse when I'm stressed, but I have to study for my exams at the moment. Any [1]*ideas* what to do?

Jan: I'm [2]_____ I can't really help you. Have you [3]_____ about asking Ed?

Liz: That's a good idea. I'll be seeing him later. Oh, wait. There he is now. Ed! Over here!

Ed: Hi, girls! How are things?

Jan: Well, I'm fine, but Liz here keeps getting headaches. I'm not sure what she should do.

Liz: That's right. Jan recommended I speak to you. What do you [4]_____?

Ed: You [5]_____ take a painkiller.

Liz: I'd prefer not to, if possible. I don't really like taking medicine.

Ed: Well, maybe you don't drink enough water. It might be a good [6]_____ to carry a bottle around with you.

Liz: Like this, you mean? I drink loads of water!

Ed: Hmm … Well, I don't know what else to suggest, I'm afraid. If I [7]_____ you, I [8]_____ make an appointment to see the doctor.

Liz: Yes, I think I will do that.

I can use quantifiers to talk about activities and sports.

1 Decide if the pairs of sentences are the same (S) or different (D).

1 ☐ I don't have any of the medals.
I have none of the medals.

2 ☐ James is ill. Susan is ill.
Both James and Susan are ill.

3 ☐ Gail has a sore throat. Anna doesn't have a sore throat.
Neither Gail nor Anna has a sore throat.

4 ☐ Luke likes abseiling, but he doesn't like snowboarding.
Luke likes both abseiling and snowboarding.

5 ☐ Vegetables, fruit, salad and eggs: these are good for you.
Vegetables, fruit, salad, eggs. All the food listed is good for you.

6 ☐ You can ask Jim, but you can't ask Jo.
You can ask either Jim or Jo.

2 Choose the correct option.

1 Have you ever done (any)/ none extreme sports?

2 Sandra's neither fit nor / or healthy.

3 I didn't like neither / either of the films we watched.

4 You can have either / or soup or a sandwich.

5 I've taken none / any of the medicine yet.

6 Both Jess and Tom like / likes their doctor.

3 Complete the dialogues with one word in each gap.

1 A: I feel sick.
B: I'm not surprised. You've eaten _all_ the cake and the chocolate!

2 A: Where shall we all go for your birthday?
B: Well, I'd like to have pizza, but _____ Jenny nor Amanda like pizza.

3 A: The shop has five new types of cakes. Have you tried _____ of them?
B: No, I've tried _____ of them.

4 A: Who ate _____ the biscuits?
B: It wasn't me!

5 A: Did you ask your brothers if they can come to the party?
B: Yes, _____ Mark and James can come!

4 Complete the second sentence so it has the same meaning as the first one. Use the words in brackets.

1 Jack has hay fever. Gary has hay fever. (both)
Both Jack and Gary have hay fever.

2 I didn't eat any of the sandwiches. (none)
I _____ the sandwiches.

3 Sue hasn't got a temperature. She hasn't got a rash. (neither)
Sue has got _____ a rash.

4 You can have a party or you can go out for dinner. (either)
You can _____ go out for dinner.

5 My mum doesn't like broccoli. My sister doesn't like broccoli. (nor)
Neither my mum _____ broccoli.

6 I play lot of different sports at school and I enjoy every sport. (all)
I enjoy _____ we play at school.

5 Read the text. Choose the correct answers.

Very extreme sports

Abseiling, sandboarding, bungee jumping – [1]**all** of these are extreme sports, but [2]____ of them is a *very* extreme sport.

What about volcano surfing? Despite the name, you can do this [3]____ on a volcano or on a mountain. You'll need [4]____ a helmet and a special suit though, as it's very dangerous. You can reach speeds of up to eighty kilometres per hour!

Then there's crocodile bungee – jumping into and out of water full of crocodiles! But [5]____ volcano surfing nor crocodile bungee seem as scary as cliff-diving. This is where you jump off a cliff into water, using [6]____ of the protective equipment of other extreme sports.

Would you try [7]____ of these? I certainly wouldn't. I'm neither adventurous [8]____ crazy!

1	a	both	(b)	all	c	none	d	neither
2	a	either	b	any	c	none	d	nor
3	a	neither	b	or	c	either	d	all
4	a	either	b	and	c	all	d	both
5	a	nor	b	neither	c	either	d	both
6	a	none	b	any	c	both	d	either
7	a	any	b	nor	c	none	d	neither
8	a	or	b	and	c	either	d	nor

For each learning objective, tick (✓) the box that best matches your ability.

😊😊 = I understand and can help a friend.

😊 = I understand and can do it by myself.

☹ = I understand but have some questions.

☹☹ = I do not understand.

		😊😊	😊	☹	☹☹	Need help?	Now try ...
6.1	Vocabulary					Students' Book pp. 70–71 Workbook pp. 66–67	Ex. 1–2, p. 75
6.2	Grammar					Students' Book p. 72 Workbook p. 68	Ex. 3, p. 75
6.3	Reading					Students' Book p. 73 Workbook p. 69	
6.4	Grammar					Students' Book p. 74 Workbook p. 70	Ex. 4, p. 75
6.5	Listening					Students' Book p. 75 Workbook p. 71	
6.6	Speaking					Students' Book p. 76 Workbook p. 72	Ex. 6, p. 75
6.7	English in use					Students' Book p. 77 Workbook p. 73	Ex. 5, p. 75

6.1   I can talk about health problems.
6.2   I can report what somebody else has said.
6.3   I can understand specific detail in different types of text.
6.4   I can use reported speech to talk about commands and requests.
6.5   I can listen for specific detail and talk about extreme sports.
6.6   I can ask for and give advice.
6.7   I can use quantifiers to talk about activities and sports.

What can you remember from this unit?

New words I learned (the words you most want to remember from this unit)	**Expressions and phrases I liked** (any expressions or phrases you think sound nice, useful or funny)	**English I heard or read outside class** (e.g. from websites, books, adverts, films, music)

Vocabulary

1 Complete the sentences with the words below.

> abseiling   allergy   bug   hay fever   injury
> travel sickness

1 Every summer it's the same: my _____ makes me sneeze all day!
2 Scott got a bad _____ when he was playing football last week.
3 Take this medicine. It will stop you getting _____ when you're on the boat.
4 I can't eat that. I have a food _____.
5 The doctor said I have that _____ that's going round at the moment.
6 I tried _____ once, but I was too scared to climb down the wall.

2 Write words using suffixes.

1 the noun from *operate* _____
2 the adjective from *asthma* _____
3 the adjective from *stress* _____
4 the adjective from *pain* _____
5 the noun from *sick* _____

Grammar

3 Read the dialogue. Then complete the text reporting the conversation. Use one word in each gap.

John: Excuse me, my appointment was half an hour ago and I'm still waiting to see the doctor.

Receptionist: I'm sorry, sir. The doctor is very busy today. I'll call you when he's ready to see you. Do you want a coffee while you wait?

John: No, thanks. I don't feel well. When will the doctor be ready to see me?

Receptionist: I'm sorry, sir, I don't know.

John told the receptionist that his appointment [1]_____ been half an hour before and he [2]_____ still waiting. The receptionist apologised and said the doctor [3]_____ very busy [4]_____ day. She said she [5]_____ call him when he was ready and asked him if he [6]_____ a coffee while he waited. John said he [7]_____ feel well and asked when the doctor [8]_____ be ready to see [9]_____. The receptionist said she [10]_____ know.

4 Rewrite the commands and requests in reported speech. Use *told* or *asked* and the words in brackets.

1 'Stay in bed.' (doctor / me)
_____

2 'Can you help me change my bandage, please?' (I / my friend)
_____

3 'Take this medicine twice a day'. (nurse / him)
_____

4 'Please be quiet.' (Sally / us)
_____

5 'Don't touch that.' (Kevin's mum / him)
_____

5 Choose the correct option.

1 *Both / All* James and Karen have injuries after the match.
2 Neither Sally *nor / or* Tina has any homework to do.
3 I ate *none / any* of the cookies. Honest!
4 Have you got *any / all* food allergies?
5 You can ask *either / neither* Graham or Ben to help you.

Speaking language practice

6 Complete the dialogues with the words below. There are two extra words.

> advice   any   could   going   good   if
> know   something   would   you

1 A: What's the matter, Ben?
   B: I've burnt my hand. _____ ideas what to do?
   A: If I were _____, I'd put it under a cold tap.
   B: Good idea. Thanks.

2 A: I've got this pain in my leg. What's your _____?
   B: I wish I could suggest _____, but I can't. It might be a _____ idea to see a doctor.

3 A: So, if you were me, what _____ you do?
   B: I'd recommend _____ to see the school nurse. I don't really _____ what to advise myself, I'm afraid.

1 Match 1–6 with a–f to make phrases from the text.

1	b	be prone to	a indoors
2	☐	be allergic	b allergies
3	☐	suffer	c a rash
4	☐	get	d treatment
5	☐	stay	e from hay fever
6	☐	receive	f to pollen

2 Complete the sentences with the correct form of the phrases from Exercise 1.

1 My sister *is prone to allergies* and she often sneezes if there is a strong smell such as perfume or smoke in a room.

2 I have to _____ a lot in spring because of my hay fever. If I go outside, I sneeze a lot and get a runny nose.

3 Many people who _____ also have asthma and breathing difficulties.

4 If you _____ , then you mustn't have flowers in your room!

5 The doctor told me that I might _____ on my arms and legs if I lie down in the grass.

6 If you don't _____ for an allergy attack in time, it can be quite dangerous.

3 Rewrite the statements in reported speech using *say* or *tell*.

1 'I am allergic to eggs and nuts.' (Helen / tell me)
   Helen told me (that) she was allergic to eggs and nuts.

2 '20,000 people have been sent to hospital because of allergies.' (the report / say)
   _____

3 'I developed asthma very late in life.' (she / say)
   _____

4 'Children will represent half of all new cases.' (the journalist / tell us)
   _____

5 'You can become allergic even if your parents didn't have any allergies.' (the expert / say)
   _____

4 Match questions 1–3 with pictures A–C.

1 ☐ Are we allergic to our own homes?

2 ☐ Should we go back to being more natural and being outside?

3 ☐ Will Emma get an allergic reaction?

5 Choose the correct option.

The TV programme included an experiment which looked ¹(*closely*)/ *deeply* at the lives of allergic families. It showed that if you come into ²*touch* / *contact* with something you're allergic to, you can get a serious reaction. For example, when Emma does a test at the hospital, she gets an itchy ³*epidemic* / *bump* on her arm. This happens because our ⁴*allergy* / *immune* system overreacts. These allergic attacks are not normally serious. However, if you have a severe reaction, you can get a drop in ⁵*breathing* / *blood pressure*.

6 Complete the sentences with the verbs below.

dig   hold   pick up   ~~put~~   reconnect   trigger

1 The doctor *put* small amounts of different foods on Emma's arm.

2 Changes to our surroundings may _____ the key to the rise in allergies.

3 Some food – like fish, nuts and eggs – can _____ an allergic response.

4 Dogs often like to _____ around in the dirt.

5 If we spend more time outdoors, we will _____ organisms which can help to fight bacteria.

6 Studies suggest that we need to _____ with good bacteria.

7 Read the video script. Underline any words or phrases you don't know and find their meaning in your dictionary.

Part 1: An allergy epidemic

Narrator: We are in the middle of an allergy epidemic. This is Morgan. He is allergic to many foods – eggs, nuts, dairy products and bananas – dogs and cats, horses, pollen, dust and even latex. One in three of us
5 suffer from allergies, like eczema, asthma or hay fever, and they send more than 20,000 of us to the hospital every year.

To find out why, in this programme we are going to look closely at the lives of some allergic families. We want to know why so many of us are becoming allergic. To understand this, we need to understand what
10 happens during an allergic reaction. Whatever it is that triggers the response, whether it's eggs, nuts or dust mites, the reaction in the body is very similar.

Doctor: So, first of all, I'm just going to write some marks on here – one, two, three …

15 Narrator: Today Emma is at the hospital for some allergy testing. The doctor is putting small amounts of different foods on her arm and checking if there is a reaction. They want to find out exactly what she is allergic to.

Doctor: Let me know if it hurts. I'll be as gentle as I can.

Narrator: If you are allergic to eggs, for example, when you come into contact
20 with them, your immune system starts to overreact.

Doctor: If there is an allergy, what would normally happen is what's called a 'wheel-and-flare' reaction, which is a little itchy bump with some redness around it.

Narrator: But if you're unlucky and you have a more severe reaction that we
25 refer to as 'anaphylaxis', then it could involve difficulty in breathing, so particularly, wheeziness. Another severe reaction can be a drop in blood pressure and that can be very serious indeed.

Part 2: A healthier future

It is difficult to say exactly what is behind the allergy epidemic. Although genes are important, it's becoming increasingly clear that changes to our environment may also hold the key to the rise in allergies. And as scientists around the world start to discover exactly what these changes are, it's giving hope for children like Morgan in the future.

Like the families, perhaps the best thing all of us can do to improve our health and reduce the risk of allergies is simply reconnect with good bacteria and micro-organisms. We need this good bacteria to fight off the bad bacteria. It is this good bacteria that we evolved with.

This is Harry the cocker spaniel. He's helping his owners to find all sorts of insects. It's true that dogs, not humans, like to dig around in the dirt but we can learn something from our dogs' behaviour.

Harry picks up all sorts of interesting organisms from the environment while digging holes.

Studies suggest that reconnecting with bacteria in the natural world is good for our health. We can't all have dogs but there are other ways to get outside more and spend more time in green spaces, no matter how small they may be.

A clear message

VOCABULARY
Non-verbal communication | Word building: verbs and nouns for communication | Advertising

GRAMMAR
The Passive: Present Simple, Past Simple, Present Perfect, *can* and *must* | The Passive with *will*

READING
True or false

LISTENING
Listening for the main points in an interview

SPEAKING
Giving compliments

WRITING
A review

BBC CULTURE
Why do languages change?

I can talk about different forms of communication.

1 ● Choose the correct option.

1 It's important to have good *posture / head movements* if you sit down for a long time every day.
2 My mum always uses a lot of *voice / gestures* when she speaks. She looks like an orchestra conductor!
3 In my country, we generally don't like a lot of *body contact / facial expressions*. We like to have personal space.
4 I sometimes think I have no control over my *head movements / facial expressions*. People can always tell what I'm thinking!
5 People say I have a nice *voice / body contact* and it makes them feel calm.
6 Depending on their *head movements / eye contact*, I can tell if someone agrees or disagrees with me.

2 ●● Complete the puzzle. What is the mystery word?

1 what you use to speak or sing
2 use these to show you agree or disagree with something
3 the position you hold your body
4 when you touch a person, e.g. putting your arm around someone
5 how you express different emotions with your face
6 how you move your hands
7 looking into someone's eyes

3 🔵 **WORD FRIENDS** Complete the phrases with the verbs below.

| bow   give   ~~nod~~   point   raise   shrug

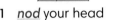

1 _nod_ your head

2 _____
your eyebrows

3 _____
your shoulders

4 _____

5 _____
someone
a hug

6 _____
a finger

4 🔵🔵 Complete the sentences with one word in each gap.

1 James, you're shaking your _head_. Do you disagree?
2 _____ me in the eye and tell me it wasn't you who said those things about me.
3 Always make eye _____ with the customer. It shows you are interested in them.
4 Lisa could tell I was surprised because I raised my _____.
5 Lower your _____. This is a library.
6 I find it difficult to read facial _____.
7 Don't _____ your shoulders – say 'I don't know.'
8 Hey you! Come here, _____ me a hug!

5 🔵 Complete the sentences with the noun form of the verbs in brackets.

1 People from different cultures use different forms of non-verbal _communication_ (communicate).
2 Fiona's studying for her exams. She needs to work without _____ (interrupt).
3 We had an interesting _____ (discuss) in class today about different cultures.
4 There's a lot of _____ (repeat) in your essay. Try to think of some new ideas.
5 I use an app to help me with my _____ (pronounce) of new words in English.
6 Check in the dictionary for the correct _____ (define) of this word.
7 What shall we get Janine for her birthday? Do you have any _____ (suggest)?

6 🔵🔵🔵 Read the text. Choose the correct answers.

Getting by in a foreign country

When I travel to another country, I always try to learn the language so I can ¹___ with local people. I don't just study words and grammar, but ²___ too, so people can understand me. However, this isn't always possible, especially if you're just going somewhere for a short holiday. It's amazing how much you can express with gestures and ³___ expressions. Looking somebody in the ⁴___ and ⁵___ your eyebrows is important because it shows you're paying attention to what they're saying. If you don't understand someone, stay calm and don't raise your ⁶___ – there are better ways to show you don't understand. One ⁷___ is to simply ⁸___ your shoulders in a friendly way and smile. Be careful with some gestures though as they can mean different things around the world. If you ⁹___ your head in Bulgaria, it actually means 'yes'. And in some countries it's rude to point a ¹⁰___ at other people.

1 a communicate   b communication
   c discuss   d discussion
2 a speak   b pronounce
   c pronunciation d repetition
3 a face   b head
   c voice   d facial
4 a mouth   b eye
   c face   d head
5 a raising   b nodding
   c pointing   d moving
6 a head   b gestures
   c body   d voice
7 a suggest   b suggestion
   c definition   d define
8 a shake   b lower
   c shrug   d bow
9 a point   b shake
   c shrug   d lower
10 a body   b hand
   c head   d finger

7.2 GRAMMAR The Passive

I can use verbs in the Passive.

1 ● Complete the sentences with the Passive form of the verbs in brackets.

1 Billions of emails *are sent* every day. (send – Present Simple)

2 Mobile phones _____ for years. (use – Present Perfect)

3 The message _____ by James. (not write – Past Simple)

4 Mobile phones _____ in class. (turn off – must)

5 Ball games _____ here. (play – can't)

6 My stolen bike _____ yet. (not find – Present Perfect)

2 ● Choose the correct option.

Last Tuesday our class ¹(were sent)/ have been sent to a workshop on improving our communications skills. We were told ²by / for our teachers that it would be fun. They were right! We played several games in pairs and small groups. These are special games – they ³can be designed / have been designed to make us communicate without speaking. They must ⁴be / been played using gestures or body contact only. I like it when we ⁵were given / are given workshops like this at school which can ⁶be / are substituted for other classes. It makes the day much more interesting!

3 ●● Use the prompts to write sentences in the Passive.

1 **photographs / can / not / take / in here**
Photographs cannot be taken in here.

2 this picture / was / paint / Monet
_____

3 the audio guide / can / listen to / on your mobile phone
_____

4 **tickets / must / buy / at the ticket office**
_____

5 this sculpture / was / make / a 1,000 years ago
_____

4 ●● Rewrite the sentences in the Passive.

1 They speak English in India.
English is spoken in India.

2 They make mobile phones in China.
_____

3 They haven't taught Latin in our school for years.
_____

4 You can show your pictures on the big screen.
_____

5 You must write your answers on this form.
_____

6 They haven't made any good films this year.

5 ●●● Complete the text with the phrases below. There is one extra phrase.

> are given   are recorded   are swapped   are shown
> ~~can be done~~   has been answered   have been designed
> must be taught   were lost   weren't taught

Teaching communication skills

What ¹**can be done** to teach communication skills in school? The question ²_____ by one school in the north of England. At Saint Andrew's School, teachers believe that students ³_____ how to communicate properly. They have special classes where students ⁴_____ how to introduce themselves, how to give presentations and the importance of eye contact. These classes started last year, when teachers noticed some students were having difficulties in speaking exams. Marks ⁵_____ in exams because of communication problems.

Since then, a number of additional workshops ⁶_____ to help students practise these communication skills. One of the activities the pupils ⁷_____ is to prepare a short presentation. Students ⁸_____ by their partner using a mobile phone. The phones ⁹_____ and they give each other feedback. Students find it useful when they get feedback from another student, rather than the teacher or the whole class, because it creates a safe environment.

I can understand a text about communication between different people.

1 Read the texts. Which person would say these things?

1 'I prefer speaking to my friends online.' _____

2 'I want you to be more like I was.' _____

Pamela

When I was a child, I was always told, 'Children should be seen and not heard.' But I was a chatty girl and I used to fire questions at my parents all the time. It would drive them mad! I remember on special occasions all the family used to get together and I was told to sit down and be quiet. I was a bit of a rebel though and always shouted out things I shouldn't! I think the reason I was like this was because I was an only child – I didn't have any brothers or sisters. If I had had a brother or sister to play with, then I wouldn't have been so annoying for my parents, I don't think. My son is an only child too, but he doesn't behave the way I did. Instead, he's always on his mobile phone, texting his friends or playing games. Sometimes when I see my son with his eyes stuck to his mobile phone, it makes me feel sad and I wish he was a bit more 'annoying' like I used to be! I feel as if he's missing out on the opportunities I had to go out and really communicate with people. He's become a bit of a 'screenager' – you know, a teenager who's always looking at his phone.

Ben

People think I don't like to talk much and my mum thinks I'm shy, but that's not true. She thinks that I always spend time on my mobile phone or my computer. I've been told to go out and meet people so many times, it drives me mad! Don't get me wrong – it's not that I don't like talking to my friends, it's just that I don't see why we should all have to go and meet somewhere when we can do it on the phone or via an app. We can all chat together and send photos and videos. We can also meet new people on social networking sites, so it's actually a lot more sociable than communicating face-to-face. My mum thinks I spend too much time 'on my own', but in fact, I think I'm more sociable than her!

2 Read the texts again. Mark the sentences T (true) or F (false).

1 ☐ Pamela used to talk a lot when she was a child.

2 ☐ She didn't have anyone her age to talk to at home.

3 ☐ She thinks her son goes out with his friends too much.

4 ☐ Ben is very talkative at home.

5 ☐ He thinks it's unnecessary to meet his friends face-to-face to talk to them.

6 ☐ He only talks to people he knows online.

3 Which person:

1 gets annoyed when he/she is told to do something? _____

2 did something he/she shouldn't have?

_____

3 wants someone else to be more chatty?

_____

4 doesn't see why face-to-face communication is important?

_____

5 worries about the way someone else communicates? _____

6 thinks you can do more things online than face-to-face? _____

I can change active sentences into passive sentences.

1 ● Match 1–6 with a–f to make sentences.

1 [c] Exam results will
2 [ ] The speech will
3 [ ] The school's future will
4 [ ] Katy's suggestion will
5 [ ] Your parents will
6 [ ] Homework will

a be given every day at the end of class.
b be decided by the education committee.
c be posted on the school website.
d be emailed about the school trip.
e be given by the ex-president.
f be discussed at the next meeting.

2 ● Complete the sentences using the Passive with *will*.

1 Important information about the workshop *will be sent* (send) by email next week.
2 Careers advice _____ (give) during the workshop.
3 You _____ (teach) how to improve your communication skills.
4 Mobile phones _____ (not allow) during the workshop.
5 A question and answer session _____ (hold) at the end.
6 You _____ (not test) during the workshop at all.

3 ●● Complete the sentences using the Passive with *will* and the verbs below.

| give   not offer   not use   send   ~~show~~   win

1 Students *will be shown* how to apply for college.
2 The writing competition _____ by the person who writes the most interesting story.
3 These extra classes _____ to all students – only those who have failed speaking exams.
4 You _____ a text message with an access code. Use this to change your password on the website.
5 Peanuts _____ in this recipe as some people may have a food allergy.
6 A prize _____ for the best presentation.

4 ●●● Complete the text using the Passive with *will* and the verbs below. There are two extra verbs.

| ask   ~~choose~~   discuss   give   organise   publish   read

● ● ●

New student president

Next month a new student president [1]*will be chosen* by you, the students. Anyone who wishes to be student president must write a short text about why they think they should be president. The texts [2]_____ by the teachers. After that, they [3]_____ in the school magazine. On the day of the election, students [4]_____ a form to complete with the name of the candidate they want to choose. The winning candidate [5]_____ to give a short speech. Good luck!

5 ●●● Look at the signs and notices. Write sentences using the Passive with *will* and the verbs in brackets.

We're sorry but the shop won't be open tomorrow because we're redecorating.
Come back on Friday!

1 (close) *The shop will be closed tomorrow.*

New courses!

We have a range of new courses for the next school year.
Come in and ask us about them.

2 (offer) _____

Party for all students, Friday 8 July
Let's celebrate the end of the school year together!

3 (organise) _____

Class meeting – things to discuss:
1 new class president
2 school trip
3 Greentime project

4 (discuss) Three _____

FX900 Smartphone – the wait is nearly over!
In shops from 3 September

5 (sell) _____

I can understand key information in short dialogues about advertising.

1 Choose the correct option.

1 I hate it when I'm watching a film and it's interrupted every fifteen minutes by *billboards* / *commercials*.
2 Sam's got a part-time job giving out *slogans* / *flyers* in the High Street.
3 Who is our target *audience* / *poster* for the product?
4 What's your favourite *brand* / *logo* of soft drink?
5 I'm not sure about the new *logo* / *slogan*. I think it looks old-fashioned.

2 Complete the crossword.

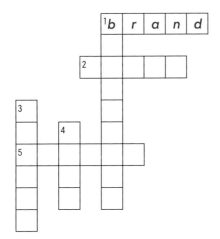

Across

1 the name of a particular kind of product made by one company
2 a piece of paper advertising an event or product
5 a short, easy to remember, phrase used in advertisements

Down

1 a large sign outside which is used for advertising
3 a printed picture or photograph advertising something which is put up in a public place
4 a small design or word which is the official sign of a company

3 🔊 15 Listen to five extracts from TV commercials. Match commercials 1–5 with products a–h. There are three extra products.

a ☐ washing powder
b ☐ soap
c ☐ pizza
d ☐ chocolate
e ☐ party planning service
f ☐ headphones
g ☐ cleaning service
h ☐ shampoo

4 🔊 16 Listen to four short conversations. Choose the correct answers.

1 What time is Jitesh's garage sale?

2 What do the football academy offer for free if you sign up for a summer course?

3 What do you get free in the supermarket offer?

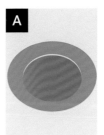  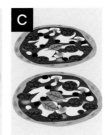

4 What do you have to wear for the burger offer?

5 🔊 16 Listen again. Mark the sentences true (T) or false (F).

1 ☐ Jitesh wrote the wrong time on his poster.
2 ☐ Gary got a free T-shirt from the football academy.
3 ☐ The pizzas on offer are very small.
4 ☐ You can get fries at Zoom's.

I can indicate different objects, ask for and give clarification.

1 Match 1–6 with a–f to make sentences.

1 [e] That's
2 [ ] Which one
3 [ ] It's the
4 [ ] Those are the ones which
5 [ ] What I was trying
6 [ ] When you said 'LOL',

a I didn't like.
b what did you mean?
c do you mean?
d to say was that they're not popular these days.
e it!
f one that has a pink logo.

2 Order the words to make phrases.

1 mean / left / did / you / ?
Did you mean left?

2 said / meant / green, / blue / I / I / when
_____

3 here / these / ones
_____

4 that / you / could / again / say / ?
_____

5 meant / sorry, / I / say / right / to
_____

6 these / at / look / !
_____

3 Write the phrases from Exercises 1 and 2 in the correct column.

Indicating objects	Asking for clarification	Giving clarification
That's it!		

4 Match 1–2 with a–c to make phrases. There is one extra ending.

OUT of class

1 [ ] Any idea where
2 [ ] That's a

a bit tricky!   c the toilets are?
b much easier!

5 Complete the dialogues with the phrases from Exercise 4.

1 A: _____
   B: Yes, downstairs, on your left.
2 A: I'm trying to do my homework on the bus.
   B: _____

6 🔊 17 Complete the dialogue with one word in each gap. Listen and check.

Assistant: Good afternoon. How can I help you?
Clara: I'm looking for a new laptop. The problem is I don't know anything about them. I basically want to use it for doing my homework and chatting to my friends.
Assistant: I see. Well, these ones [1]*here* are popular.
Clara: Which ones do you [2]_____? They look like tablets.
Assistant: Sorry, I [3]_____ to say the laptops behind you.
Clara: Oh, [4]_____ ones here?
Assistant: That's them. So, they come with all the programs you need for homework and one TB of memory.
Clara: Um … when you [5]_____ 'one TB', what did you [6]_____?
Assistant: Oh sorry, when I said 'one TB', I [7]_____ 'one terabyte'. What I was [8]_____ to say is that this is a lot of space on the computer to keep files like your homework, videos, songs, photos, etc.
Clara: OK, that sounds good. Can I have a look?
Assistant: Of course. Here you are.

I can write a review and offer opinions and points of view.

1 Choose the correct option.

1 Unfortunately, it looks quite ~~confusing~~/ *easy* to use. The instructions aren't clear either.

2 It looks *awful / fantastic* – it's very attractive and has a shiny black cover.

3 I was impressed by how *useful / poor* it is. It really does the job when you need it.

4 For a mobile game, it's quite *impressive / boring*. You spend a lot of time just waiting for your character to move along each level.

5 The only *disappointing / fun* thing about the website is that you have to pay to use it, and it's not cheap.

2 Read the review. Is it a positive or negative review overall?

Phonix: the new pronunciation app

There are hundreds of apps out there for language learning, so how can we know which ones are good? [1]*Lots of people have asked me about* Phonix, the pronunciation app, so I decided to write a review. [2]_____ how easy it is to use. I was playing with it seconds after I'd downloaded it. [3]_____ by the games on it too. Some of them are fantastic and really fun to play. I could play them for hours! [4]_____, the design is a bit disappointing. The screens are quite boring and there aren't many pictures. [5]_____ it's an impressive app. If you don't mind the awful design, then it's worth the money. [6]_____ language learners.

3 Complete the review with phrases a–f.

a I was impressed

b I would definitely recommend it to

c All in all, I think

d Lots of people have asked me about

e Unfortunately

f I particularly like

4 Put the information in the order it appears in the review.

a ☐ Say what you like and don't like.

b ☐ Give your personal opinion and make a recommendation.

c ☐ Say what you are reviewing and why you chose to review it.

5 Choose the correct option. Then decide if the sentence belongs in a, b or c from Exercise 4.

1 ☐ The *just /* ⟨*only*⟩ disappointing *thing / things* about the app is the cost.

2 ☐ Phonix is one of the *most / more* popular apps on the market, but is it as good *like / as* they say?

3 ☐ This is one of the best *app / apps* I have ever *used / used ever*.

6 Complete the notes about an app with the words below.

confusing   design   remembering   sounds
useful   ~~vocabulary~~

Wordit app

Type of app: [1]*vocabulary* **recorder**
What I liked:
- fantastic [2]_____ – very beautiful fun games
- very [3]_____ for learning and [4]_____ vocabulary

What I didn't like:
- [5]_____ to use at times, instructions aren't clear
- [6]_____ and music on it are awful

Recommend it? Yes!

7 Look at the notes in Exercise 6. Write a review of the app. Follow the instructions below.

1 Use the review in Exercise 2 as a model.

2 Include the following in your review:
- what you are reviewing and why you are reviewing it
- what you like and dislike about it
- your personal opinion and whether you would recommend it to others.

3 Use adjectives from Exercise 1.

4 Use phrases from Exercises 3 and 5.

For each learning objective, tick (✓) the box that best matches your ability.

☺☺ = I understand and can help a friend.

☺ = I understand and can do it by myself.

☹ = I understand but have some questions.

☹☹ = I do not understand.

		☺☺	☺	☹	☹☹	Need help?	Now try ...
7.1	Vocabulary					Students' Book pp. 82–83 Workbook pp. 78–79	Ex. 1–3, p. 87
7.2	Grammar					Students' Book p. 84 Workbook p. 80	Ex. 4, p. 87
7.3	Reading					Students' Book p. 85 Workbook p. 81	
7.4	Grammar					Students' Book p. 86 Workbook p. 82	Ex. 5, p. 87
7.5	Listening					Students' Book p. 87 Workbook p. 83	
7.6	Speaking					Students' Book p. 88 Workbook p. 84	Ex. 6, p. 87
7.7	Writing					Students' Book p. 89 Workbook p. 85	

7.1 I can talk about different forms of communication.

7.2 I can use verbs in the Passive.

7.3 I can understand a text about communication between different people.

7.4 I can change active sentences into passive sentences.

7.5 I can understand key information in short dialogues about advertising.

7.6 I can indicate different objects, ask for and give clarification.

7.7 I can write a review and offer opinions and points of view.

What can you remember from this unit?

New words I learned (the words you most want to remember from this unit)	**Expressions and phrases I liked** (any expressions or phrases you think sound nice, useful or funny)	**English I heard or read outside class** (e.g. from websites, books, adverts, films, music)

Vocabulary

1 Choose the correct option.

1 Have you seen that huge *billboard / flyer* in the High Street? It's looks awesome!

2 Give Roshan some space – he doesn't like *posture / body contact*.

3 People with autism find it difficult to read other people's facial *expressions / gestures*.

4 Have you seen the *slogan / flyer* I got in the music shop?

5 I know it sounds strange, but I like watching *logos / commercials*.

6 Don't raise your *posture / voice* at me!

2 Complete the sentences with the correct form of the words below.

> communicate define describe discuss explain interrupt repeat suggest

1 Please don't _____ me while I'm speaking.

2 Look in the dictionary for a clear _____ of the word.

3 Sorry, could you _____ that? I didn't hear you the first time.

4 You _____ the place so clearly it feels like we're there ourselves!

5 We need to have a _____ about your school work.

6 That's a great _____. OK then, let's do that.

7 At school we have special classes to improve our _____ skills.

8 I don't understand what you mean. Can you _____?

3 Match 1–6 with a–f to make phrases.

1 ☐ shrug   4 ☐ shake
2 ☐ give   5 ☐ raise
3 ☐ look   6 ☐ point

a your head
b somebody a hug
c your shoulders
d a finger
e somebody in the eye
f your voice

Grammar

4 Rewrite the sentences in the Passive. Use *by* if necessary.

1 Our Maths teacher gave us lots of homework.
We _____.

2 They play football in Brazil.
Football _____.

3 They have advertised their new product on billboards.
Their new product _____.

4 You must follow the rules at all times.
The rules _____.

5 You can't take photos in here.
Photos _____.

6 Flyby has announced a new flight to Ireland.
A new flight to Ireland _____.

5 Complete the text. Use the Passive with *will*.

The government has announced today that 100 new technical schools [1]_____ (open) across the country. A range of modern courses [2]_____ (offer) by each school. Also, students [3]_____ (teach) how to drive by qualified driving instructors and basic car repairs [4]_____ (include) in the course too. The schools [5]_____ (build) using recyclable materials and they [6]_____ (locate) in poorer areas of the country, where education standards are lower than the rest of the country.

Speaking language practice

6 Complete the dialogues with one word in each gap.

A A: Which one do you [1]_____? This one [2]_____?
  B: No, that's [3]_____ old one.
  A: Ah, [4]_____ one over there?
  B: That's [5]_____!

B A: I live at 42 Caldwell Street.
  B: Sorry, [6]_____ you say that again?
  A: Yes, it's 42 Caldwell Street.

C B: [7]_____ you texted 'TTYL', what did you mean?
  A: What I was trying to [8]_____ was, 'Talk To You Later.'

D A: Did you mean those ones [9]_____ have the blue cover?
  B: That's [10]_____!

1 Match 1–6 with a–f to make Word Friends.

1 c global   a terms
2 ☐ digital   b varieties
3 ☐ colloquial   c language
4 ☐ business   d tongue
5 ☐ language   e technology
6 ☐ mother   f meetings

2 Complete the sentences with the Word Friends in Exercise 1.

1 English is a *global language* because so many non-native speakers use it.
2 New _____, like Taglish, are being created all the time.
3 In _____, it is not unusual for there to be no native speakers present at all.
4 Thanks to _____ like apps and websites, more people can study English.
5 Some people think that _____, like 'innit?' are not acceptable.
6 340 million people around the world speak English as their _____.

3 Rewrite the sentences in the Passive. Use *by* where necessary.

1 Non-native speakers have transformed English.
   English *has been transformed by non-native speakers*.
2 People coin new phrases all the time.
   New _____.
3 In some countries, a lot of people must speak English as a second language.
   English _____.
4 We will create more and more language varieties in the future.
   More and more language varieties
   _____.
5 Digital technology has introduced many new terms into our vocabulary.
   Many new terms _____.

4 Use the prompts to write sentences.

1 they / be / here / because / they / can get good quality teaching
   They are here because they can get good quality teaching.
2 Taglish / speak / on the streets of Manila
   _____
3 many new words / introduce / into English recently
   _____
4 some people think 'lol' / not be / a real word
   _____

5 Match photos A–D with sentences 1–4 from Exercise 4.

6 Choose the correct option.

1 A lot of *governments* /(*foreigners*) travel to the Philippines to study English.
2 The Filipinos are the third largest English-*speaking* / *spoken* nation in the world.
3 Most university *courses* / *topics* are taught in English in the Philippines.
4 'Chav' is an example of a *text* / *slang* word that's been coined recently.
5 We couldn't understand what he was saying because his *conversation* / *accent* was so strong.
6 *LOL* and *IMO* are examples of *media* / *textspeak*.

7 Complete the sentences with the correct form of the verbs below.

| attract   coin   count   include   mix   t̶r̶a̶c̶k̶ |

1 The Global Language Monitor *tracks* words across the media.
2 Do you think it's possible to _____ all the words in the English language?
3 De La Salle University _____ students from all over the world.
4 Some people think that we shouldn't _____ slang words in the dictionary.
5 Who first _____ the term 'textspeak', do you think?
6 'Taglish' is English with some of the local language Tagalog _____ in.

8 Read the video script. Underline any words or phrases you don't know and find their meaning in your dictionary.

Part 1: Learning English abroad

Teacher: Have you guys heard of the words 'first impressions'?

Presenter: Ahed Al-Khayat is learning English in the Philippine capital Manila. Ahed is from Saudi Arabia but his classmates are from Taiwan, Libya and Japan. Other students are from Belgium and Brazil. They're all here because they can get good quality teaching for a fraction of what it would cost in America or the United Kingdom.

Ahed: Everybody here speaks English very well. The accent is very good and it is a cheap place to stay and learn.

Presenter: There are about a 100 million people in the Philippines, most of whom speak at least some English. The government proudly states that this is the third largest English-speaking nation in the world and that's sort of true.

Presenter: Hello, sir. Can I have a coconut, please?

Seller: How many, madam?

Presenter: Just one, thanks.

Seller: OK.

Presenter: That kind of English that he just spoke there is typical all through the Philippines. It's English but with the local language, Tagalog, mixed in – it's more like Taglish than English. And that must make it quite difficult for foreigners who are studying English here to know what's English and what's Philippine English. But this hasn't deterred people from coming here. Every year the number of foreign students goes up. Immigration data shows there are three times as many now than there were just three years ago. And the Philippines doesn't just attract students who want to learn English. Elizaveta Leghkaya already speaks it. She's come here from Russia to do an engineering degree and language isn't a problem because most courses at the top Philippine universities are taught entirely in English.

Elizaveta: Here it's much cheaper compared to other countries. I also checked about Australia and New Zealand but it's too much. So my parents can't afford it.

Presenter: Do you think that the education level is the same here?

Elizaveta: Sure, I think De La Salle is a very good education, seriously!

Presenter: This university firmly believes the teaching it provides can match up to that anywhere in the world. And with the cost of being a student rising every year and the competition for jobs tougher than ever, it's not surprising that more and more people are looking further afield for good quality cheap education.

Part 2: What is a word?

What makes a word a word? Well, that all depends on who you ask. We asked these people to write the words they don't like in black and the words they do like in red. Do you think, for example, that 'chav' is a word?

Some people said that it is not because it's slang. But what makes a word a word then? Are slang words words? Should they be in the dictionary?

Some people think they should be because they are used in everyday vocabulary. And they are part of our culture now.

Anything that you use in a conversation that somebody else gets the meaning of is a word.

Is 'innit' a real, proper word?

It means something so, in that respect, it would be a proper word.

How about 'LOL' – laugh out loud – and other textspeak?

Everyone uses 'LOL' because it's fun and it represents funniness! But should they be in the dictionary though?

The American company The Global Language Monitor has a system that tracks words across the media. It says we have more than a million words in the English language now. This is controversial though, and some critics question their calculation methods. By the way, if you want to compare, the *Oxford English Dictionary* has around 300,000 entries, including *chav* and *blog*.

Expert: A word becomes a word when it's used by one person and understood by another. But really, a word needs to be used in enough different resources. We need to see evidence of its use in a wide variety of resources; monitor it electronically. It could be in print, it could be in speech but we need to find hard evidence of its usage for it to be included in the dictionary.

8

Creative energy!

VOCABULARY
Art | Literature and books | Art and literature | The press

GRAMMAR
Ability | Obligation and prohibition

READING
Multiple choice

LISTENING
Listening for specific details

SPEAKING
Comparing ideas and expressing opinions

ENGLISH IN USE
Phrases with prepositions

BBC CULTURE
Graffiti: street art or vandalism?

I can describe works of art and talk about books.

1 ● Write the words below in the correct column.

abstract contemporary graffiti graphic art illustration
landscape oil painting pop art portrait sculpture
sketch still life watercolour

Types of art	Types of paintings/drawings
abstract	

2 ● Match words from Exercise 1 with photos A–F.

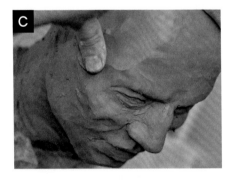

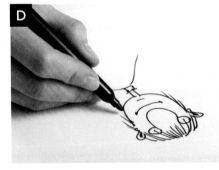

3 ●● Choose the correct option.

1 I love the *graffiti* / *illustrations* in this children's book.

2 Do you like my *sketch* / *oil painting*? I did it with that pencil you bought me.

3 Andy Warhol was a famous artist who created *pop* / *life* art.

4 *The Mona Lisa* is one of the most famous *landscapes* / *portraits* of all time.

5 I don't really like contemporary *art* / *sculpture*. I much prefer the classical stuff.

4 ● Match the words below with the definitions. There is one extra word.

autobiography chapter character cover
novelist ~~playwright~~ plot poem scene

1 someone who writes stories for the theatre _____ ***playwright***

2 a book someone writes about their life _____

3 the story of a book, play or film _____

4 a person in a book, play or film _____

5 a section of a book _____

6 someone who writes long stories _____

7 a short text with short lines that expresses emotions _____

8 part of a play where there is no change in time or place _____

5 ●● Complete the words in the sentences.

1 Lord Byron was a famous nineteenth-century **p o e t**.

2 I prefer reading **n _ n-f _ _ _ _ _ n** books to **f _ _ _ _ n**. I like to read about things which actually happened.

3 I love the **i _ _ _ _ _ _ _ _ _ _ n** on this book cover.

4 Who was the **a _ _ _ _ r** of *War and Peace*?

5 I'm reading a great crime **n _ _ _ l** at the moment.

6 Jane is performing in the school **p _ _ y**. This year they're doing *Romeo and Juliet*.

7 Have you read the **b _ _ _ _ _ _ _ y** of Muhammad Ali? It's really interesting.

8 Some people say that **g _ _ _ _ _ _ i** done on walls isn't art, but I disagree.

6 ● WORD FRIENDS Match 1–8 with a–h to make phrases.

1 [b] promote   a in the news
2 [ ] get   b your work
3 [ ] win   c an exhibition
4 [ ] hold   d a speech
5 [ ] give   e a painting
6 [ ] do   f bad reviews
7 [ ] appear   g a novel
8 [ ] write   h an award

7 ●● WORD FRIENDS Complete the text with one word in each gap.

How to become famous

So you've [1]***written*** a novel or a play, or maybe
[2]_____ a portrait. What's the best way to
[3]_____ your work? Well, if you have lots of
work to show, you could hold a(n) [4]_____. If it's
something you've written, you could [5]_____ a
reading, describing your work and the story. If you
appear in the [6]_____, then this might help you
[7]_____ good reviews. Ultimately, of course, the
best way to get ahead is to win a(n) [8]_____.

8 ●●● Complete the texts with one word in each gap.

One of my favourite [1]***playwrights*** is Bola Agbaje. She is
very talented and every [2]_____ she has written has
won a(n) [3]_____. She writes urban comedies and
lots of the [4]_____ are set in modern-day London.
Her first play, *Gone Too Far!* has lots of lively, realistic
[5]_____, who are a pleasure to watch. It has now
been made into a film.
Charlotte

One of my favourite modern artists is Damien Hirst.
Nowadays, his [6]_____ art is well-known around
the world, but it wasn't always that way. He came
from quite a poor family. He started promoting his
[7]_____ early on, when he held an independent
[8]_____ which he organised with some friends. It
[9]_____ good reviews and appeared in the
[10]_____. Charles Saatchi, an advertising
executive, visited this show and offered to pay Hirst
to create anything he wanted. He has [11]_____
many important awards, including the Turner Prize.
Steve

I can talk about ability in the present, past and future.

1 ● Match 1–6 with a–f to make sentences.

1 [c] I couldn't
2 [ ] Sheila can
3 [ ] Unfortunately, Keith won't
4 [ ] Will you be able
5 [ ] We can't
6 [ ] I managed

a read in five languages!
b offer you a place at our college, I'm afraid.
c understand the French film – they all spoke very fast.
d to find the book you wanted.
e to finish the book this week?
f be able to come to the party.

2 ● Choose the correct option.

1 (Were) / *Did* you able to ride a bike when you were five?
2 Ben and Kate won't *be able* / *able* to come to the play.
3 Can you *write* / *to write* poetry?
4 I *managed* / *manage* to read fifteen books over the summer!
5 The theatre was so full of people that we *couldn't* / *could* see the stage.
6 I started writing a novel, but I didn't *manage* / *manage to* finish it.

3 ●● Choose the word or phrase which does NOT fit each sentence.

1 ___ to speak to your mum last night?
  a Did you manage   b Were you able
  ⓒ Could you
2 I ___ post that letter for you – sorry.
  a can't   b managed to
  c won't be able to
3 I ___ read when I was three, but only slowly.
  a can   b could   c was able to
4 I ___ drive, but I'm taking lessons.
  a can't   b 'm not able to
  c managed to
5 The book was difficult to follow, but I ___ finish it.
  a couldn't   b was able to
  c managed to
6 Unfortunately, Gary ___ finish his homework on his own.
  a didn't manage to b wasn't able to
  c managed to

4 ●● Cross out the extra word in each sentence.

1 I can't ~~to~~ speak for very long – I need to finish my homework.
2 Sarah missed the start of the play because she didn't wasn't able to leave on time.
3 I'll be able to can finish all my homework before 6 p.m.
4 I wasn't didn't manage to finish the design for our club T-shirts.
5 Can you really able finish a book in one day?
6 She couldn't be concentrate because she didn't sleep well last night.
7 Can he manage study and text his friends at the same time?
8 She isn't can't able to come with us this evening because she's got to study.

5 ●●● Find and correct six mistakes in the text.

● ● ●

Thank you,
Ms Palmer!

When I was younger, I wasn't very good at anything. I couldn't swim, I ~~won't be~~ able to read very well and I couldn't ride a bike on my own until I was twelve! People used to ask me things like, 'Can you to say "thank you" in French?' and I just looked down and felt embarrassed. The problem was I just didn't have any confidence. I could to do these things if I really tried, but I didn't believe I could. Then one day I had a new French teacher, Ms Palmer, and she gave me lots of attention. She really encouraged me and said things like, 'If you manage read this text, I'll let you play the French app on your tablet for ten minutes.' It worked and not only did my French improve, but now I'm able do lots of other things and I feel more confident too. Next year I'm hoping I was able to learn Spanish and Italian too. 'Merci beaucoup, Ms Palmer!'

1 *wasn't*   4 _____
2 _____   5 _____
3 _____   6 _____

I can identify detail in a text about a street art tour.

1 Read the text quickly. Does the writer enjoy the tour?

Shoreditch delights

It's 10 a.m. on a cold London morning and I'm here in Shoreditch, East London, with Ragel, our tour guide. We're taking a tour of the area, but this is no ordinary tour. We won't be able to find out about the historical buildings or famous people from the past. We're here to find out about the street art in the area.

'There's always something new,' says Ragel. 'It's a very dynamic art world. Because space is limited, you can't expect to see the same piece on a wall forever. Other street artists will come and paint over it. If you manage to keep a painting up on a wall for more than a few months, it's because other artists really respect your work.'

Ragel tells us a bit about the different types of art we see. He points out 'paste-ups', which are ready-made pictures that artists stick to walls to save time. Someone makes the mistake of talking about 'graffiti'. Ragel gets a bit annoyed and says that graffiti is messy, people writing their names. This isn't graffiti.

This is street art. To show what he means, he then takes us down the road and points to a shop, covered in a beautiful picture of a woman's face. 'That one there,' he explains, 'was painted by a local artist called Zhen. The shop owner was annoyed because people used to just write graffiti all over the shop, so she paid Zhen to paint a picture. Now nobody writes on it out of respect.'

The tour includes lots of photo stops. Ragel is also a photographer and shows us how to get the best shots of street art. While people are taking photos, he explains to me that street art has brought a lot of money into what was once a poor area. In the past, most tourists only visited famous places, but with all the street art here, Ragel and others have managed to bring business to Shoreditch by holding tours and exhibitions.

I had a great day and I managed to get some great photos. I recommend Ragel's tour to anyone who's interested in 'dynamic art'.

2 Read the text again. Choose the correct answers.

1 What does the writer try to do in this text?
   a Describe all the different types of street art in Shoreditch.
   b Give a review of a street art tour.
   c Show how to paint street art.
   d Apologise for describing street art as 'graffiti'.

2 Why is it a 'dynamic art world', according to Ragel?
   a Because the art changes quite quickly.
   b Because there isn't much space.
   c Because the paintings are so good.
   d Because people respect the work street artists do.

3 Why does Ragel get annoyed when someone calls it 'graffiti'?
   a Because he doesn't like the people who create graffiti.
   b Because graffiti isn't dynamic.
   c Because he had an argument with a shop owner.
   d Because he doesn't think graffiti is art.

4 Ragel believes his street tours have
   a taken people to famous places.
   b been good for the local area.
   c taught him how to be a good photographer.
   d helped his own art skills.

3 Find words or phrases in the text with these meanings. The words appear in the same order as the sentences.

1 an item of art   *piece*
2 create a picture on top of another one so it hides the first one _____
3 prepared at an earlier time   _____
4 not tidy or organised   _____
5 photos   _____

I can talk about obligation and prohibition in the past, present and future.

1 ● Decide if the pairs of sentences are the same (S) or different (D).

1 [S] You must do your homework tonight.
 You have to do your homework tonight.
2 [ ] We mustn't use our mobile phones in here.
 We don't have to use our mobile phones in here.
3 [ ] Jake had to wear a shirt.
 Jake was allowed to wear a shirt.
4 [ ] They'll have to clean up the street.
 They won't be allowed to leave any litter.
5 [ ] I didn't have to pick up my little brother.
 I wasn't allowed to pick up my little brother.
6 [ ] She won't have to study all evening.
 She'll be allowed to have a break.

2 ● Complete the text with the words below.

| allowed aren't ~~don't~~ must mustn't

There's an unusual exhibition on at the art gallery in town. To start with, it's free. Well, you ¹**don't** have to pay anything, but you can if you want to. Another unusual thing is that you ²_____ write in a little book at the end to give your opinion on the exhibition and you ³_____ write more than three words. I've never seen anything like this before. The exhibition is interesting because you are ⁴_____ to touch the pieces in the gallery. You can pick them up, throw them around, even break them! But you ⁵_____ allowed to say bad things about them. It's quite weird, but interesting, I think.

3 ●● Choose the correct option.

1 You *mustn't / didn't have to* leave so early last night.
2 Do you *must / have to* sing that song all the time? It's really annoying!
3 You *don't have to / mustn't* wear a shirt, but you can if you want to.
4 I *had to / was allowed to* work really hard to pass that exam.
5 I *wasn't / won't be* allowed to come with you – my parents never let me do anything!

4 ●● Complete the second sentence so it has the same meaning as the first one. Use the words in brackets.

1 I'll have to go to bed early tonight. (allowed)
 I *won't be allowed* to stay up late tonight.
2 To do this activity, you have to ask three other students the questions. (must)
 To do this activity, you _____ three other students the questions.
3 They didn't have to leave. (were)
 They _____ stay.
4 You mustn't talk during the play. (aren't)
 You _____ during the play.
5 Were you allowed to go out on your own when you were younger? (have)
 _____ go out with an adult when you were younger?

5 ●●● Complete the text with one word in each gap.

A tale of two schools

My last school was very unusual because there were almost no rules. We were ¹**allowed** to wear what we wanted (there was no uniform) and we did ²_____ have to do any homework. In fact, we didn't ³_____ to go to class if we didn't want to! But we ⁴_____ to respect each other and no fighting or bullying was allowed.

My new school is completely the opposite. We ⁵_____ do all our homework and if we don't do it, we ⁶_____ to do double homework as a punishment. We ⁷_____ not allowed to wear anything we want – we have ⁸_____ wear a school uniform. But they are thinking about changing this rule next year, so we ⁹_____ have to wear a school uniform. But we will still ¹⁰_____ to wear smart clothes. We won't ¹¹_____ allowed to wear jeans and trainers, for example.

6 Choose the correct option.

OUT of class

1 What's *on / up*? You look worried.
2 Sorry I'm *late / lately*. I missed the bus and had to walk here.
3 Remember: this isn't dangerous. Just jump and don't be scared. Off we *are / go*!

I can understand an interview about the press.

1 Match the words below with the definitions.

celebrity gossip   editor   headlines   magazine   paparazzi   ~~tabloid~~

1 a newspaper which has lots of photos and celebrity news instead of serious news stories _tabloid_

2 news about famous people which may or may not be true _____

3 a large but thin book which has stories and photographs and is published every week or month _____

4 the head of a newspaper or magazine who decides what stories are published _____

5 titles of newspaper reports _____

6 photographers who take photos of famous people to sell to newspapers _____

2 Choose the correct option.

1 My aunt is a (journalist) / paparazzi. She writes stories for one of the main national newspapers.

2 I never read the national / local news. It's always just stories about a lost cat or something unimportant like that.

3 Would you like me to read your horoscope / celebrity gossip for you? It's always true, you know!

4 I don't buy newspapers any more. I just read the news on an online news site / a broadsheet.

5 When you've finished writing the article, send it to our reporter / designer who will style it on the page.

6 I hate it when I'm watching a film and it's interrupted by commercials / weather forecasts.

3 🔊 18 Listen to an interview with an editor. What is *The Weekly Voice*?

a a student newspaper which became a national newspaper

b a school newspaper covering news about the school Naomi attends

c a student newspaper which publishes stories about teachers at the school

4 🔊 18 Listen again. Mark the sentences T (true) or F (false).

1 ☐ *The Weekly Voice* won a famous prize recently.

2 ☐ The newspaper is written by experienced professional journalists.

3 ☐ At first, the school didn't mind what stories they wrote.

4 ☐ Naomi chose to print the story about the teacher.

5 ☐ They became a national newspaper with no help from anyone else.

5 🔊 18 Match 1–8 with a–h to make sentences. Listen again and check.

1 ☐ *The Weekly Voice*
2 ☐ Naomi Smith
3 ☐ At first, the school
4 ☐ Miguel
5 ☐ The school principal
6 ☐ All of the students
7 ☐ Tabloid and broadsheet newspapers
8 ☐ The editor of a national newspaper

a wrote a story about one of the teachers that he'd seen outside school.

b won the prestigious Nigel Thompson Award for best new journalism.

c had lots of rules about what they could publish in the newspaper.

d visited the school.

e wasn't happy when Naomi decided to publish the story about the teacher.

f gave *The Weekly Voice* advice and some money.

g is the editor of the newspaper.

h complained when the newspaper was shut down.

6 Match words/phrases 1–4 from the listening with definitions a–d.

1 ☐ prestigious
2 ☐ gone from strength to strength
3 ☐ the secret of your success
4 ☐ closed us down

a become more and more successful

b respected; one of the most important

c made us stop

d the reason you are so successful

I can compare and contrast ideas and express a personal opinion.

1 Choose the correct option.

1 If you (ask) / tell me, I think it's a bad idea.
2 In my *thinking / opinion*, it's amazing.
3 *Personally, / On my own,* I think rap is more interesting than rock music.
4 I'm not *sure / know* which is best.
5 This magazine is exactly the same *as / so* the one I usually buy.

2 Complete the sentences with the words below. There are two extra words.

> concerned far from one other see
> seems wrong

1 As far as I'm **concerned**, it doesn't matter what we do.
2 I could be _____, but I think he's a Biology teacher.
3 Paparazzi are totally different _____ other types of photographers.
4 It _____ to me that we're not looking at all the possibilities.
5 On the _____ hand, it doesn't taste as good, but on the _____ hand, it's much cheaper.

3 Write the sentences from Exercises 1 and 2 in the correct column.

Comparing and contrasting ideas	Expressing an opinion
_____	*If you ask me.*
_____	_____
_____	_____
_____	_____

4 Complete the sentences with one word in each gap.

1 A BBQ is the *best* idea for the party because everybody likes burgers.
2 The problem, as I _____ it, is that the book was boring, so the film won't be any better.
3 Do you know what? I think you're _____ and I was wrong.
4 As _____ as I can see, there's no reason not to write a rap song about snakes!
5 I think this film is _____ the same as the one we watched last week!

5 Complete the dialogues with phrases a–c.

> a Sort of   b I bet   c see how it goes

1 A: _____ you could write a really good song if you tried.
   B: Do you think so?
2 A: Do you think we'll be hungry when we get home? Shall I buy some food?
   B: I don't know. Let's just _____.
3 A: Do you think this is a good magazine?
   B: _____. They have some good articles, but there are a lot of adverts in it.

6 🔊 19 Complete the dialogue with one word in each gap. Listen and check.

Victoria: So, which song do you think should win the school talent contest, Rob?

Rob: What a difficult decision! In [1] *my* opinion, they're all really good.

Victoria: I know, right? On the one [2]_____, I really like Sula's song about her boyfriend who moved away, but [3]_____ the other hand, Jonny's rap about his pet snake was funny!

Rob: Exactly. It seems to [4]_____ that we need to decide if we go for the emotional one or the funny one.

Victoria: Well, [5]_____ I see it, Sula's song is totally different from Jonny's. I [6]_____ think Jonny's is very musical, to be honest.

Rob: I see what you mean. I'm not [7]_____ which is better though.

Victoria: I know. It's difficult to choose.

Rob: OK, well, if you [8]_____ me, I think we should choose Jonny's rap. It's funny and original.

Victoria: I think you're [9]_____. Shall I tell him or do you want to?

Rob: You can if you want.

1 Complete the diagrams with *at*, *by*, *in* or *on*.

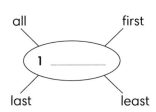

all   first

1 _____

last   least

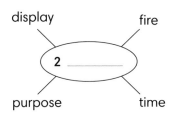

display   fire

2 _____

purpose   time

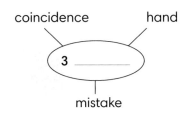

coincidence   hand

3 _____

mistake

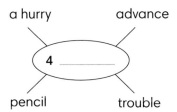

a hurry   advance

4 _____

pencil   trouble

2 Choose the correct option.

1 Sorry, the book you want is (on) / *in* loan to another student.

2 If you don't start studying soon, you'll be *on* / *in* danger of failing the exam.

3 I think I just deleted all your messages *by* / *on* mistake!

4 *At* / *By* last! I thought you were never going to get here!

5 I don't like this film *at* / *on* all.

6 These books are all *on* / *in* sale at the moment.

7 I didn't mean to wear the same shirt as you. It was purely *by* / *on* coincidence!

8 Sorry I didn't say hello to you the other day. I was *on* / *in* a hurry to get to school.

3 Look at the pictures. Choose a word from A and a word from B to complete the sentences.

A
at   by   in   on

B
fashion   fire   first   hand

1 _____, James wasn't sure if he could paint, but now he paints with confidence.

2 You're doing brilliantly, Antonia. You're _____!

3 All our furniture is made _____, sir.

4 Jonathan never likes to wear clothes which are _____.

4 Complete the text with one preposition in each gap.

BOOKSWAP

[1]*At* last! A new website which allows you to discover new books for free! Introducing Bookswap, the popular new service based in the UK. There are no costs [2]_____ all and you'll never be [3]_____ danger of having nothing to read. If you have a book you've finished reading and want to swap it for something new [4]_____ a hurry, then just register on the website. You then look for other users online and see what books they have to offer. Their books will be [5]_____ display in their virtual 'bookcase'. When you have chosen what you want, send the user a message and offer them a book of your own. We recommend writing a note [6]_____ hand and putting it inside the book for a personal touch. You have control of the design of your own virtual bookcase, so don't leave it [7]_____ a mess!

For each learning objective, tick (✓) the box that best matches your ability.

☺☺ = I understand and can help a friend.   ☹ = I understand but have some questions.

☺ = I understand and can do it by myself.   ☹☹ = I do not understand.

		☺☺	☺	☹	☹☹	Need help?	Now try ...
8.1	Vocabulary					Students' Book pp. 94–95 Workbook pp. 90–91	Ex. 1–2, p. 99
8.2	Grammar					Students' Book p. 96 Workbook p. 92	Ex. 3, p. 99
8.3	Reading					Students' Book p. 97 Workbook p. 93	
8.4	Grammar					Students' Book p. 98 Workbook p. 94	Ex. 4, p. 99
8.5	Listening					Students' Book p. 99 Workbook p. 95	
8.6	Speaking					Students' Book p. 100 Workbook p. 96	Ex. 6, p. 99
8.7	English in use					Students' Book p. 101 Workbook p. 97	Ex. 5, p. 99

8.1 I can describe works of art and talk about books.
8.2 I can talk about ability in the present, past and future.
8.3 I can identify detail in a text about a street art tour.
8.4 I can talk about obligation and prohibition in the past, present and future.
8.5 I can understand an interview about the press.
8.6 I can compare and contrast ideas and express a personal opinion.
8.7 I can understand and use phrases with prepositions.

What can you remember from this unit?

New words I learned (the words you most want to remember from this unit)	**Expressions and phrases I liked** (any expressions or phrases you think sound nice, useful or funny)	**English I heard or read outside class** (e.g. from websites, books, adverts, films, music)

Vocabulary

1 Choose the correct option.

1 Nobody has lived in this house for years. It's covered in *graffiti / oil paintings*.

2 Sit still and try not to move while I paint your *landscape / portrait*.

3 *The Times* is a *broadsheet / tabloid* newspaper which has serious articles and fewer photos.

4 Before I paint a picture, I always draw a *watercolour / sketch* with a pencil first.

5 This is Gemma, our *journalist / designer*. She makes sure every page looks just right before we print.

6 Have you checked the *weather forecast / horoscopes*? You might need an umbrella today.

7 When I'm in a hurry, I just read the *adverts / headlines* to find out what's happening in the news.

8 I couldn't follow the *plot / scene* of that film – it was too complicated.

2 Write the correct word for each definition.

1 someone who writes long stories
   n _ _ _ _ _ _ _

2 a book about someone's life, which someone else writes   b _ _ _ _ _ _ _ _

3 something you watch in a theatre   p _ _ _ _

4 a person who writes a book   a _ _ _ _ _ _

5 a book with a fictional story   n _ _ _ _ _

6 a person who writes pieces for the theatre
   p _ _ _ _ _ _ _ _ _

Grammar

3 Complete the sentences with the correct form of the words in brackets.

1 I _____ (not able/visit) Charlotte yesterday.

2 _____ (you/able/return) this book to the library tomorrow?

3 I _____ (not can/swim) when I was four.

4 _____ (you/manage/finish) your painting?

5 They _____ (not able/go) on holiday next year.

6 I _____ (not can/speak) Russian.

4 Choose the correct option.

1 A: What *do we have to / we must* do for homework?
   B: We don't *have / have to* do anything tonight!

2 A: *Did / Were* you allowed to stay up late when you were little?
   B: Oh no. I *had / have* to be in bed by 7 p.m.

3 A: Sorry, I'll have *to leave / leave* at 4.30 p.m. today.
   B: It's OK, you *didn't / won't* have to stay later than that, anyway.

4 A: *Is / Does* Jake allowed to come on holiday with us?
   B: Only if his parents say he *is allowed to / has to* come.

5 A: You *must / must to* buy a ticket before you get onto the bus.
   B: Oh, I *don't have to / am not allowed to* buy a ticket. I have a monthly pass.

5 Complete the phrases with *at, on, by* or *in.*

1	_____ advance	6	_____ mistake
2	_____ ink	7	_____ loan
3	_____ foot	8	_____ purpose
4	_____ least	9	_____ trouble
5	_____ display	10	_____ last

Speaking language practice

6 Complete the dialogue with one word in each gap.

Alice: What's your favourite kind of art, Felipe?

Felipe: I'm not sure. [1]_____ the one hand I like modern art, but on [2]_____ other hand, some classical art is just brilliant.

Alice: I know what you mean. [3]_____ my opinion, classical portraits are amazing – the way the eyes follow you! Actually, it [4]_____ to me that a lot of modern art is just nonsense.

Felipe: Oh, I don't know. As I [5]_____ it, modern art is [6]_____ different from classical art. You just can't compare the two.

Alice: Maybe. But as far as I'm [7]_____, modern art is just silly. I don't enjoy it all.

Felipe: Well, if you [8]_____ me, you just haven't really seen much of it.

1 Match 1–6 with a–f to make phrases from the text.

1	[a] real	**a**	identity
2	☐ tourist	**b**	work
3	☐ early	**c**	attraction
4	☐ local	**d**	walls
5	☐ main	**e**	streets
6	☐ concrete	**f**	council

2 Complete the sentences with the phrases from Exercise 1.

1 Nobody knows Banksy's _real identity_ – it's a total mystery.

2 The Eiffel Tower is my favourite _____ in Paris.

3 Graffiti can look very effective on _____ .

4 There isn't much left of Banksy's _____ – it has all been destroyed.

5 The _____ in Bristol would like to keep some street art.

6 You can see lots of graffiti on Bristol's _____ .

3 Complete the sentences with the correct form of the words in brackets.

1 They _couldn't_ (can) understand why I didn't like the graffiti because they loved it.

2 We _____ (manage to) see the exhibition because we arrived too late.

3 You _____ (be able to) see the street art if the local council clean it off.

4 It's amazing that Banksy _____ (be able to) sell his work at auction – after all it's just graffiti!

4 Complete the sentences with the phrases below.

great charities   iconic work   last chance usual hype   world famous

1 Although there was the _usual hype_ surrounding the opening of the exhibition, I didn't think that it was very good.

2 A lot of Banksy's _____ has disappeared over the years.

3 Some graffiti artists have become _____ because of the internet.

4 The money which is raised from the auction will be given to some _____ which support unemployed artists.

5 This is your _____ to buy a piece at this auction – there's only one painting left!

5 Choose the correct option.

1 Does street art become /(belong) in an art gallery?

2 The workers are trying to destroy the graffiti by *spraying* / *prettying* it with chemicals.

3 Another option is simply to *print* / *paint* over it.

4 Some people think that graffiti *defeats* / *degrades* a neighbourhood.

5 Banksy has *involved* / *inspired* lots of other street artists.

6 Bristol council believes that some street art is worth *saving* / *selling*.

6 Choose the correct answers.

1 Graffiti artists use buildings as their ___ .
   a still life   **b** sculpture   **c** canvas
   d landscape

2 I think this graffiti is awful; it degrades the building and I would ___ it.
   a get rid of   **b** bet   **c** encourage   **d** save

3 This graffiti is great and it has a serious message. I ___ Banksy did it.
   a tag   **b** bet   **c** mess   **d** support

4 If the city doesn't spray away the graffiti, it will ___ people to write on walls and there will be more and more sprayed walls in our city.
   a degrade   **b** bet   **c** make   **d** encourage

5 The ___ from the auction are going to a charity supporting artists.
   a funds   **b** mess   **c** canvas
   d councils

7 Complete the text with the correct form of the phrases below.

be able to   can   mustn't   ~~not be allowed to~~ not have to

In the past, you [1]_weren't allowed to_ paint on walls in my town, even if it was artistic. It was completely illegal. Now, in some parts of the city, you [2]_____ paint graffiti on walls. There are special places which encourage street art. But you [3]_____ paint any tags. If you're interested, you can learn to do street art yourself in workshops. You [4]_____ have any experience. Next month, you [5]_____ see an exhibition of street art in the city centre. Why not go along and check it out?

8 Read the video script. Underline any words or phrases you don't know and find their meaning in your dictionary.

Part 1: Graffiti in Bristol

Presenter: Off it comes. Bristol's graffiti busters spray away at another illegal tag. But will they soon have rather less to do? The council here says some street art is worth saving. Bristol is the home of Banksy, who's inspired a whole generation to use the streets as a canvas. But what should stay and what should go?

Man 1: Personally, I think it degrades the neighbourhood a bit. That's my opinion.

Presenter: So you'd say it should go?

Man 1: Well, I wouldn't like to see that on the front of my house.

Woman 1: Someone's just written a word on a wall and sort of prettied it up a little bit.

Presenter: So you'd get rid of that one?

Woman 1: I'd get rid of that one. Paint over it.

Presenter: OK. What about that one?

Woman 1: This is absolutely fantastic. It's a beautiful piece of art and I think anyone would be happy to have that on their wall.

Presenter: I bet they wouldn't!

Woman 1: Well, I would be happy to have it on my wall.

Presenter: Should it stay or should it go?

Man 2: No, I think that's just a mess that is, yes.

Presenter: Bristol has become world famous for this kind of thing, but will saving the best of it just encourage even more?

Part 2: Banksy's auction

Presenter: Bansky in Beverley Hills. It doesn't sound quite right, does it? And in the end it wasn't. But the evening began with the usual hype. As ever with Banksy, there are more questions than answers. Does street art like this belong in an auction? If you own the bricks, do you own the soul of the work? And what does the artist make of all this?

Auctioneer: One of the premier Banksy pieces you can take home. An iconic work straight out of Detroit. Take it home today in Beverley Hills!

Presenter: And there were Banksy bargains galore.

Auctioneer: Your last chance. Any interest? All right, and we're selling it at the back of the gallery for $110,000.

Buyer: What I love is that it came out of Detroit. It came out of the US. And the funds are going towards a great charity to support artists so ... I like it even better now that I know the story.

Presenter: This mural was also on sale. The BBC first filmed it on a wall in Bethlehem. It's now in London, but who was selling it and how they got it is not clear. In any case, the two big Banksys here went for less than a third of what the sellers had hoped for. Perhaps this undercover art is now overexposed?

9

Let's get together

9.1 VOCABULARY Celebrations

I can talk about special occasions.

1 ● Read the descriptions and complete the words for celebrations.

> We make breakfast in bed for my mum and give her a card and flowers.

1 M o t h e r ' s D a y

> We invited friends round to celebrate in our new home.

2 h _ _ _ _ _ -w _ _ _ _ _ _ _ p _ _ _ _

> The community leader said some words and then we all prayed together.

3 r _ _ _ _ _ _ _ _ c _ _ _ _ _ _ _

> We had a party on Jamie's last day at our school to wish him luck.

4 l _ _ _ _ _ _ _ p _ _ _ _

> On my birthday, a few friends came round and we had a nice meal.

5 d _ _ _ _ _ p _ _ _ _

> On 31 December my parents invited lots of friends to our house and we danced until the morning.

6 N _ _ Y _ _ _ _ E _ _ p _ _ _ _

2 ●● Complete the sentences with one word in each gap.

1 My sister had her wedding *reception* in the local community centre.
2 Every year in September we have a cultural _____ in my town where we celebrate the food that was grown in the summer.
3 At the end of the year I'm taking my girlfriend to the school _____ .
4 Last weekend we had a big family _____ and I saw my uncle who I hadn't seen for five years!
5 I love getting presents on my name _____ . It's like a second birthday!

3 ● **WORD FRIENDS** Match 1–7 with a–g to make Word Friends.

1 [c] celebrate   a a street party
2 [ ] bring   b the tradition of your culture
3 [ ] turn   c a birthday
4 [ ] follow   d good luck
5 [ ] make   e a toast
6 [ ] put up   f eighteen
7 [ ] throw   g decorations

4 ⬤⬤ Complete the sentences with the words below. There are two extra words.

> candles   ceremony   eighteen   ~~eve~~   family   hired
> off   present   reception   school   street   toast
> unwrapped   warming

1 Last year we had a New Year's *Eve* party and we let _____ fireworks in the garden.
2 My friend moved house last week. I'm wrapping a(n) _____ to take to her house-_____ party.
3 Sally and her friends _____ a limo to take them to the _____ prom last year.
4 This year we're having a big _____ get-together to celebrate my cousin turning _____.
5 At the wedding _____, the bride's father made a(n) _____ to the happy couple.
6 Chris's birthday was great. After he _____ his presents, we brought out a cake and he blew out the _____.

5 ⬤ Match the words below with photos 1–5.

> flag   national symbol   parade   public holiday
> ~~traditional costume~~

1 *traditional costume*

2 _____

3 _____

4 _____

5 _____

6 ⬤⬤ Choose the correct option.

1 A: Happy New ⟨Year⟩/ *Years*! How did you celebrate?
  B: We watched the *spectators* / *parade* in the square, then let off *fireworks* / *candles* in the evening.
2 A: I didn't realise tomorrow was a *public* / *family* holiday. No school for us!
  B: I know, and it's great because it's my birthday too!
  A: Oh! *Happy* / *Cheers* birthday!
3 A: Can you see what's happening? I can't see over all the *spectators* / *display*.
  B: Yes, two women in traditional *custom* / *costume* are raising the *parade* / *flag*.
4 A: Are you going to watch the fireworks *display* / *costume* later?
  B: I can't. My sister's just moved into a new apartment and she's having a house-warming *party* / *reception*.

7 ⬤⬤⬤ Complete the text with one word in each gap.

⬤ ⬤ ⬤

My day

In our family, we have a special celebration which I don't think any other family has, called 'My Day'. On [1]*New* Year's Eve, we have a family [2]_____-together and my father [3]_____ a toast to us all. We then each choose one day that year which will be 'My Day', and we have a special 'public [4]_____' on that day. When your 'My Day' comes, everyone says 'Congratulations! [5]_____ My Day!' to that person and gives them presents and a cake with candles. The person then [6]_____ out the candles and [7]_____ their presents. In the evening, we have a dinner [8]_____ for all the family and some friends and afterwards we have a firework [9]_____ in the garden. We've done this for as long as I can remember and according to my dad, it follows in the [10]_____ of his ancestors. He thinks that if we ever missed a 'My Day', it would [11]_____ bad luck.

I can be specific about people, things and places.

1 ● Mark the relative clauses D (defining) or N (non-defining).

1 [D] That's the costume which I'm wearing for the parade.

2 [ ] The New Year's parade, where I met my girlfriend, was lots of fun.

3 [ ] The band, whose music is amazing, made all the spectators dance.

4 [ ] That's the place where the parade finished.

5 [ ] The mayor, who gave a speech at the end, was really happy to see so many spectators.

6 [ ] That's the guy whose costume I borrowed for the parade.

2 ● Complete the sentences with *who*, *which*, *where* or *whose*.

1 That's the street *where* the parade will take place.

2 That's the girl _____ costume won a prize.

3 The present, _____ we bought for Clara, was made by hand.

4 The DJ, _____ music collection was all from the 1990s, wasn't very popular.

5 That's the restaurant _____ I had my birthday dinner.

6 The spectators, _____ were clearly having a good time, made lots of noise.

3 ●● Find and correct the mistakes in the sentences. One sentence is correct.

1 The limo, ~~where~~ we hired for the prom, was very luxurious inside.
   which

2 Teachers who gives lots of homework aren't usually very popular.
   _____

3 My uncle who is an engineer has never been to Ireland.
   _____

4 The party, which was to celebrate my aunt's birthday, finished quite early.
   _____

5 Paul is the student who's birthday it is today.
   _____

6 That's the house which they're having the party.
   _____

4 ●● Complete the text with one relative pronoun in each gap.

I can't wait until next week. It's our last day at school and in the evening we're having a big leaving party. This week I bought the jacket [1]*which* I'll wear to the party. I've been looking at it in the shop window for ages! The shop assistant, [2]_____ knew I wanted it, kept it to the side for me. The jacket, [3]_____ is made by hand, is really cool and fits me really well! The place [4]_____ the party is will be decorated nicely. At the party, the principal of the school, [5]_____ daughter is also leaving, will make a toast to us for the future and then we'll dance, dance, dance! I don't expect to get home until after midnight!

5 ●●● Join the sentences. Use the relative pronouns in brackets.

1 That's a man. He took our photo. (who)
   That's the man who took our photo.

2 The fireworks were fantastic. They cost a lot of money. (which)
   The fireworks, which cost a lot of money, were fantastic.

3 The leaving party went on for a long time. We ate lots of nice food there. (where)
   _____

4 My uncle is coming to our dinner party. He's a doctor. (who)
   _____

5 A house-warming party is a celebration. You have it when you move into a new home. (which)
   _____

6 Sheila is a girl. Her mother bought her a car for her birthday. (whose)
   _____

7 I am talking about Amy. She is standing next to Mark. (who)
   _____

8 This is the hotel. We had our prom here. (where)
   _____

9 Tom is my cousin. His team won the school championship. (whose)
   _____

I can find specific detail in short texts.

1 Read the descriptions and answer the questions.

Which festival(s):

1 ☐ ☐ involve a competition?
2 ☐ ☐ involve staying up all night?
3 ☐ doesn't take place in winter?

The UK's weirdest festivals

A Ap Helly Aa

This festival of fires, which takes place on the last Tuesday of January, involves a parade of torches through the streets. At the end of the parade the torches are thrown into a Viking ship, which burns in a big fire. Afterwards, the people in the parade go to local halls (e.g. schools, community centres) and perform short plays. There is then a big party for the rest of the night. It can get very cold watching the parade because it takes place in the Shetland Isles, off the north coast of Scotland. But there is lots of fire and it's free of charge to watch.

B Royal Shrovetide Football Match

This annual game, which goes back to the twelfth century, is not football as we know it. It's a modern version of 'hugball', where the ball is held more than it is kicked. It takes place on Shrove Tuesday, which is usually in February. The game is played through the whole town and the two teams, who are called the Up'ards and the Down'ards, are made up of more than 100 men, women and children!

C Cheese Rolling

This game, which takes place at the end of May, is played on Coopers Hill near Gloucester, in the west of England. A big cheese is rolled down a hill and contestants race after it (often falling over). It's a very steep hill and many contestants get injured! The winner, whose prize is the cheese, is the first person to cross the finish line. This used to be a local event, but it has now become world famous. In fact, in recent years the race has been won by an American and a Japanese man. Hundreds of spectators come to watch the game and it's a great day out.

D Winter Solstice at Stonehenge

If you are keen on spirituality and ancient history, then this is the festival for you. It takes place at Stonehenge, an ancient stone circle in south-west England. Arrive the night before, stay up until morning on the shortest day of the year and you'll see the sunrise over the stone circle. As it rises, the sun connects three of the main stones with its light – a truly unforgettable experience.

2 Three young people are coming to the UK and are each looking for a festival to attend. Match the people with festivals A–D.

☐ **Christophe**

Christophe is visiting the UK in the winter and wants to do something interesting and have fun. He wants to travel to distant places, away from the big cities. He's interested in history, especially the less well-known history of places and cultures. He likes watching parades where people wear old costumes.

☐ **Sara**

Sara is keen on astrology and ancient history. She's also really into photography, particularly taking photographs of nature. She's hoping to get some good photos to take back and show her friends and family. She's also quite adventurous and doesn't mind staying out all night to take the perfect photograph.

☐ **Shaun**

Shaun loves sport and would love to take part in a game or race when he visits the UK. He'd like to take part in a big international event with lots of people involved and would like to try something unusual. He doesn't mind doing something a bit dangerous, as long as it's exciting!

3 Find words or phrases in descriptions A–D with these meanings. The words appear in the same order as the sentences.

1 burning sticks of wood, usually carried in the hand _torches_
2 it doesn't cost anything _____
3 it takes place once a year _____
4 people who take part in a competition _____
5 going up very quickly (of a hill) _____

I can ask questions politely.

1 ● Match 1–6 with a–f to make questions. Mark the questions D (direct) or I (indirect).

1 | D | What time — | c |
2 | ☐ | Could you tell me where | ☐ |
3 | ☐ | Where | ☐ |
4 | ☐ | I was wondering what | ☐ |
5 | ☐ | Does Margaret | ☐ |
6 | ☐ | Do you have any idea if Katie | ☐ |

a is the station?
b likes Mexican food?
c do you get up in the morning?
d like Mexican food?
e the station is?
f you want for your birthday.

2 ● Choose the correct option.

1 Could you tell me what time ⟨the film starts⟩/ does the film start?
2 Do you know where *is the parade / the parade is*?
3 I was wondering *is Gary / if Gary is* keen on having a party for his birthday.
4 Do you have any idea when *Richard turns / turns Richard* twenty-one?
5 Do you know *where is there / if there is* a bank near here?
6 Could you tell me *do / if* you like broccoli?

3 ●● Order the words in brackets to complete the indirect questions.

1 Could you tell me *where the bathroom is* (bathroom / the / where / is)?
2 Do you know _____ _____ (it's / if / expensive)?
3 I was wondering _____ _____ (leaves / the bus / time / what).
4 Do you have any idea _____ _____ (arrived / the letter / if / has)?
5 Could you tell me _____ _____ (old / you / how / are)?
6 Do you know _____ _____ (are / where / Mike and Lee)?
7 Do you have any idea _____ _____ (they / are / why / arguing)?
8 I was wondering _____ _____ (address / Kevin's / you / have / if).

4 ●● Rewrite the direct questions as indirect questions.

1 Where's the party?
Do you know *where the party is*?
2 What are you doing for your birthday?
I was wondering _____.
3 Does James have a girlfriend?
Could you tell me _____?
4 How much are the tickets?
Do you have any idea _____?
5 What time did you get home last night?
Could you tell me _____?
6 Where do you go to school?
I was wondering _____.
7 Have they booked their tickets yet?
Do you know _____?
8 When is Dave coming back?
Do you have any idea _____?

5 ●●● Use the direct questions below to complete the indirect questions in the dialogue. There are two extra questions.

Are you enjoying it?
~~Could I ask you a few questions?~~
How are you going to get home?
How old are you?
Is this your first visit to the festival?
What are you going to do after it finishes?
Where do you live?

A: Excuse me. I'm doing a survey about festivals. I was wondering ¹*if I could ask you a few questions*.
B: Yes, of course.
A: Firstly, could you tell me ² _____?
B: Yes, it is.
A: Could you tell me ³ _____?
B: Oh yes. I love it!
A: And do you have any idea ⁴ _____?
B: Oh, I'm just going to go home.
A: Do you know ⁵ _____?
B: I'm travelling by train.
A: That's all. Thank you very much.
B: You're welcome.

I can identify specific detail in a radio interview.

1 Look at the pictures and write the sounds we hear.

1 _crackle_

2 _____

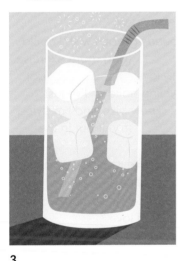

3 _____

4 _____

5 _____

6 _____

2 🔊 20 Listen to a radio interview about birthdays. Which birthday tradition do they discuss?

a singing along to famous songs
b eating birthday cake
c singing a song

3 🔊 20 Listen again. Choose the correct answers.

1 According to Scott Hurley, the song is
  a the best known song in the world.
  b the most translated song in the world.
  c the most recognised English song in the world.

2 Patty and Mildred Hill
  a composed the song for the piano.
  b first printed the song.
  c first recorded the song.

3 Most people believe that people first sang the song
  a in 1893.
  b after 1893.
  c before 1893.

4 What happens after people sing the song in Canada?
  a They sing an extension to the song.
  b They give presents to the person whose birthday it is.
  c They eat special food.

5 In Brazil, an extra part of the song refers to
  a the Portuguese language.
  b a children's character.
  c the parents of the person whose birthday it is.

6 Scott does NOT mention someone singing the song to
  a a planet.
  b a president.
  c a spacecraft.

I can use verb phrases with *to*-infinitives and *-ing* forms to talk about future plans.

1 Complete the sentences with the words below. There is one extra word.

| dying   feel   like   plans   ~~wait~~   want   wish

1 I can't *wait* to go on holiday!
2 I _____ like going out for pizza.
3 What would you _____ to do?
4 What are your _____ for the summer?
5 I'm _____ to try out my new mobile phone.
6 I _____ I could travel around the world.

2 Choose the correct option.

1 I'd love *visiting* / (*to visit*) Egypt.
2 I hope you *to have* / *have* a good time.
3 I'm looking forward to *see* / *seeing* you again.
4 I'm planning *to play* / *playing* football every day.
5 What do you fancy *doing* / *to do*?
6 I fancy *watching* / *to watch* a film.

3 Write the sentences from Exercises 1 and 2 in the correct column.

Asking about future plans	verb + noun/*-ing* form
verb + *to*-infinitive	**Other structures**
I can't wait to go on holiday!	

4 Order the words to make phrases.

OUT of **class**

a dying / for / I'm
_____

b worries / no
_____

c your / in / dreams / !
_____

5 Complete the dialogues with the phrases from Exercise 4.

1 A: My older sister's got a spare ticket for the festival. Maybe she'll give it to me.

B: _____

2 A: We've got so many exams!

B: I know. _____ the start of the holidays. Then we can take a rest!

3 A: Thanks for inviting me to the parade. It's brilliant!

B: _____

6 🔊 21 Complete the dialogue with the correct form of the verbs in brackets. Listen and check.

Em: What ¹*are* (be) your plans for the summer, Tim?

Tim: Oh, the same as usual. We're going camping.

Em: You don't sound very excited.

Tim: I'm not. I'd like ² _____ (go) on holiday with my friends, but my parents won't let me.

Em: I know what you mean. I need ³ _____ (visit) my grandparents, but I'd really love ⁴ _____ (go) to a sports camp. I fancy ⁵ _____ (play) tennis every day.

Tim: That sounds great. I wish I could ⁶ _____ (get) more exercise. I'd really love ⁷ _____ (go) on a cycling holiday. I've just bought a new bike and I'm dying ⁸ _____ (try) it out in the countryside.

Em: Can't you take it with you when you go camping?

Tim: No, we won't have enough room in the car. I'd love ⁹ _____ (take) it though.

Em: Oh dear! Well, at least we won't be at school. After all those exams I feel like ¹⁰ _____ (have) a rest!

Tim: True! Hey, I fancy ¹¹ _____ (have) an ice cream. Want to join me? My treat!

Em: That's a great idea. Thanks!

Tim: No worries. And whatever happens, I hope we ¹² _____ (have) a great summer.

Em: Me too. Here's to a great summer!

I can write an email inviting a friend to a celebration.

1 Read the email below quickly. What does Chris want Dave to do?

a go on holiday with his family

b come to a party

c go on holiday with him and his friends

2 Complete the email with the words below.

| hope   like   planning   show   speak   ~~things~~

Hi Dave,

How are ¹*things*?

I'm writing to let you know that we're going camping in August. Would you ² _____ to come? At the moment it's just Dan and me, but we hope to get at least four of us together. I know your parents want you to go camping with them, but we'll be quite near my home, so it will be safe. If you want, you can ask your mum to call mine and check. I'd really like to ³ _____ you the New Forest. We're ⁴ _____ to stay on a great little campsite with a swimming pool and near a lake.

I ⁵ _____ you can come. It would be great to see you again and I can't wait to hear your news!

⁶ _____ soon,

Chris

3 Read the email again. Mark the sentences T (true) or F (false).

1 ☐ Chris is going camping with his parents.

2 ☐ There are currently two people planning to go to the New Forest.

3 ☐ Dave's parents want him to go on holiday with them.

4 ☐ Chris wants to go swimming in the lake.

4 Put the parts of the email a–e in the order they appear in Chris' invitation.

a ☐ explaining your plans

b ☐ starting your email

c ☐ ending your email

d ☐ offering an invitation

e ☐ before you finish

5 Match a–e in Exercise 4 with phrases 1–8.

1 ☐ a ☐ I hope we can …

2 ☐ How are your summer holidays going?

3 ☐ Hope to see you soon.

4 ☐ Do you want to meet up?

5 ☐ I'm really looking forward to seeing you.

6 ☐ Let me know as soon as possible.

7 ☐ Do you fancy coming to …?

8 ☐ What have you been up to?

6 Complete the notes about Stefana's holiday with the words below.

| display   festival   go hiking   last two weeks
| ~~to email~~   with my grandmother

✎ remember ¹*to email* Liz to invite her on holiday with us

✎ where: Sicily, staying ² _____

✎ when: ³ _____ in August

✎ things to do/show her: ⁴ _____ up Mount Etna; Saint Bartholomew ⁵ _____ with fireworks ⁶ _____

7 Look at the notes in Exercise 6. Write Stefana's email inviting Liz to go on holiday with her. Follow the instructions below.

1 Use the email in Exercise 2 as a model.

2 Include these things:

 • Ask her how she is.

 • Invite her to go on holiday with you.

 • Give details about the holiday, saying what you want to do and what you want to show them.

3 Use phrases from Exercise 5.

For each learning objective, tick (✓) the box that best matches your ability.

☺☺ = I understand and can help a friend.   ☹ = I understand but have some questions.

☺ = I understand and can do it by myself.   ☹☹ = I do not understand.

		☺☺	☺	☹	☹☹	Need help?	Now try ...
9.1	Vocabulary					Students' Book pp. 106–107 Workbook pp. 102–103	Ex. 1–2, p. 111
9.2	Grammar					Students' Book p. 108 Workbook p. 104	Ex. 3, p. 111
9.3	Reading					Students' Book p. 109 Workbook p. 105	
9.4	Grammar					Students' Book p. 110 Workbook p. 106	Ex. 4, p. 111
9.5	Listening					Students' Book p. 111 Workbook p. 107	
9.6	Speaking					Students' Book p. 112 Workbook p. 108	Ex. 5, p. 111
9.7	Writing					Students' Book p. 113 Workbook p. 109	

9.1   I can talk about special occasions.
9.2   I can be specific about people, things and places.
9.3   I can find specific detail in short texts.
9.4   I can ask questions politely.
9.5   I can identify specific detail in a radio interview.
9.6   I can use verb phrases with *to*-infinitives and *-ing* forms to talk about future plans.
9.7   I can write an email inviting a friend to a celebration.

What can you remember from this unit?

New words I learned (the words you most want to remember from this unit)	**Expressions and phrases I liked** (any expressions or phrases you think sound nice, useful or funny)	**English I heard or read outside class** (e.g. from websites, books, adverts, films, music)

Vocabulary

1 Choose the correct option.

1 Would you like to go to the school *festival* / *prom* with me?

2 When my sister got married, she had a religious *party* / *ceremony* in a church.

3 Up Helly Aa is a cultural *festival* / *reception* which takes place on the Shetland Isles every January.

4 Last weekend we had a family *get-together* / *come-together* and I saw all my relatives.

5 When we moved into our new flat, we had a *house-warming* / *home-warming* party.

6 Last year my parents had a huge *New Year's Eve party* / *Mother's Day*.

7 I'd like to have a *house-warming* / *dinner* party on my birthday, but most of my friends would think it's boring.

8 Every *Mother's Day* / *dinner party*, I make my mum breakfast in bed and give her a card.

2 Complete the crossword.

Across

1 Every Christmas, we put up _____ around the house.

4 The shamrock is the national _____ of Ireland.

7 It's traditional to let off _____ on New Year's Eve.

8 Have you ever _____ a limo?

Down

2 How do you usually _____ your birthday?

3 Last year we threw a huge _____ party for the Queen's birthday.

5 At the parade, the women wore the traditional _____ of their country.

6 At the wedding, my father made a _____ to the bride and groom.

Grammar

3 Complete the sentences with *which*, *who*, *where* or *whose*. Mark the relative clauses D (defining) or N (non-defining).

1 ☐ That's the girl _____ birthday party it is.

2 ☐ The festival, _____ is held every year, attracts people from all over the world.

3 ☐ The spectators, _____ were wearing traditional costumes, clapped and cheered.

4 ☐ That's the place _____ we went for our holiday last year.

5 ☐ In Canada, _____ they sing a different version of the song, people usually make a special cake.

6 ☐ That's the man _____ daughter won the competition.

4 Use the prompts to write indirect questions.

1 could you tell me / what time / parade / start / ?
_____

2 I was wondering / where / nearest / station
_____

3 do you know / Mark / coming / party / ?
_____

4 can you tell me / how / old / you / ?
_____

5 do you know / tickets / expensive / ?
_____

Speaking language practice

5 Complete the dialogue with one word in each gap.

Nora: Yay, summer's here! What have you ¹_____ planned, Sue?

Sue: I'm planning ²_____ visit my cousin in the USA.

Nora: Wow! Really? I wish I ³_____ go there.

Sue: Why, what are your ⁴_____ for the summer?

Nora: Well, I need to ⁵_____ my grandparents at some point. But after that I fancy ⁶_____ to a concert – the Greentones are playing in August. I'm dying ⁷_____ see them!

1 Match 1–6 with a–f to make Word Friends.

1 [c] long   a costumes
2 [ ] giant   b phenomenon
3 [ ] rock   c queues
4 [ ] renowned   d concert
5 [ ] colourful   e players
6 [ ] cultural   f screens

2 Complete the sentences with the phrases from Exercise 1.

1 There are often _long queues_ to see celebrity gamers – you have to wait for ages!
2 Gaming is now a real _____. You can find it all over the world.
3 Traditional events and cultural festivals often include people dressed in _____.
4 A gaming festival is like a _____ because the big players are on stage and everybody is watching.
5 There are _____ who earn money from playing computer games online.
6 Video games are projected on _____ so everybody can see them.

3 Complete the sentences with *which*, *where* or *who*.

1 It's to celebrate video-gaming _which_ is one of the most popular hobbies in the world.
2 It's an amazing get-together _____ you can meet the world's most renowned players.
3 *Minecraft* is also everywhere, _____ shows that it's a real cultural phenomenon.
4 There are lots of fans _____ form long queues to watch celebrity gamers.
5 Stuart prefers traditional parties _____ people enjoy themselves together.
6 I've met a lot of people _____ I only knew from the internet.

4 Choose the correct option.

1 Is gaming a *legitimate* / *legal* sport?
2 The *local* / *global* audience for gaming is enormous.
3 Some famous gamers are *living* / *moving* legends.
4 Can gaming replace football as the *regional* / *national* sport?
5 Gaming is a multi-billion pound *company* / *industry*.
6 Gamers at festivals compete for big prize *money* / *awards*.
7 Playing these games requires more *sustainable* / *technical* ability than you might think.

5 Complete the sentences with the words below.

| concrete established open real |
| talented urban |

1 The dance troop is full of _talented_ kids.
2 The _____ walls of the South Bank provide a good location for BMX riders.
3 The festival aims to bring these activities out into the _____ spaces of the Southbank.
4 Painting on walls is a(n) _____ art form now – people have been doing it for years.
5 Training for a performance takes _____ dedication – you have to work hard.
6 The Southbank Festival celebrates _____ art in all its different forms.

6 Use the prompts to write sentences.

1 parkour experts / run / jump / from the concrete walls
  Parkour experts run and jump from the concrete walls.
2 he / always / dream / about / BMXing / on / ballroom floor
  _____
3 now / a youth dance troupe / rehearse / for their new show
  _____
4 next week / street artists / give / graffiti workshops / to children
  _____

7 Match photos A–D with sentences 1–4 from Exercise 6.

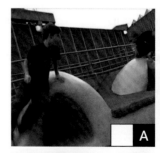 A
 B
 C
 D

8 Read the video script. Underline any words or phrases you don't know and find their meaning in your dictionary.

Part 1: The Insomnia festival

Presenter: They have come in their thousands: some to play computer games but most to watch. I know you're thinking, 'Sitting in front of a computer all day playing games is one thing but sitting watching other people playing computer games all day … really?'

5 Gamer 1: If you play the game, if you know the game, you can appreciate the level of skill and the technical ability that goes into it.

Gamer 2: It's really funny to watch some of the stuff they can pull off – and just think, 'Wow, they must really have put so much practice into this,' and it does inspire you in some way to keep on going.

Gamer 3: It's enough of a sport to be sort of sit inside and sort of hone your skills that way instead of with a

10 football or a rugby ball.

Presenter: You think it's a legitimate sport?

Gamer 3: Yeah, yeah … a legitimate sport.

Presenter: This is hi-tech professional set-up. Two teams play for thousands of pounds in prize money – you can see the tension. The game is streamed live online. There are even commentators.

15 Presenter: The global audience online and at live events last year was more than seventy million. Lost in a world of *Minecraft*, we met eleven-year old Alex.

Alex: *Minecraft* is some sort of game that is built by the perfect people.

Presenter: Why do you like watching other people playing?

Alex: Well, it makes me feel like I want to do what they are going to do.

20 Presenter: This is Josh and his mum, Michelle. Josh watches videos of gaming all the time. His mum doesn't get it.

Josh's mum: I thought it really weird and I was watching it earlier, watching people commenting on other people's playing. And I've never seen anything like it. And obviously, that's where the following is, which I hadn't really clocked – I thought it was just the gaming itself … so I do find that's slightly

25 strange.

Presenter: On stage, some living legends – gamers who record themselves playing *League of Legends* and then upload it on to YouTube. Siv has more than a million followers.

Siv: I make my living out of it and I have two employees who I am coaching to become second and third versions of me. And it's just a really nice … I'm really happy it's a sustainable job for now. Yeah.

30 Presenter: This event, Insomnia, is taking place at Coventry's football ground. So, is the national sport being overtaken by so called e-sport? Not yet. Some here can't even stay awake. But gaming is evolving and growing all the time.

Part 2: The Festival of Neighbourhood

Presenter: Spinning BMX acrobatics and Parkour experts braving the concrete walls: just some of

5 the urban art on show at the South Bank Centre Festival of Neighbourhood this weekend. Alongside them, street artists like Stick, who will be giving workshops and explaining the heritage of his trade.

Stick: People have always left their marks on walls from the periods when we were living in caves. It's a continuation of that very old tradition which is older than galleries, certainly older than

10 the Southbank. It's nice for the Southbank to be involved with such an established art form.

Presenter: There will also be a pop-up performance by youth dance troop, Zoo Nation, seen here rehearsing ahead of their new show Groove on Down the Road,' which starts at the Southbank Centre next Friday.

Dance teacher: They are, unfortunately, some of the most ridiculously talented kids that I've ever come

15 across. And I only say 'unfortunately' because for us adults, who are old, we are like watching our backs saying, 'Where have they come from? They're so good!'

Presenter: And that takes real dedication … Do you literally dance wherever you go?

Dancer 1: Pretty much, yeah … yeah … trains, at home, buses.

Dancer 2: I like it because, like, you can like express how you feel.

Dancer 3: Like we're always on our hands like all the time. We don't walk with our feet, we walk with our hands.

Presenter: Putting breakdance on a stage, taking art out of galleries and rolling BMX into the ballroom. The point of this festival is to mash up cultures and show them to a wider audience.

Festival organizer: Many of the artists that we spoke to said, 'I've always dreamt about BMXing on the ballroom floor or coming out on to the terraces or coming out on to the roof gardens.' And they really relish the opportunity to be coming into those more public and open spaces.

Presenter: The Southbank Centre has long been an unofficial playground where urban art forms are practised and honed; this weekend, a chance to see the next generation!

1 Look at the text in each question. What does it say? Choose the correct letter, a, b or c.

Tip: Use the visual information in the text (type of writing, location, etc.) to identify what type of text it is.

1

> **This bin is for glass, plastic and paper only. Please do not put non-recyclable litter into it.**

(a) This bin is for recycling only.
b This bin is for recycling and general litter.
c Do not put glass, plastic or paper in this bin.

2

> James,
> I've just been to the new climbing wall in town. It was great! Do you want to give it a go with me next weekend? Text me later today so I can book it.
> Matt

What should James do?

a tell Matt about the new climbing wall
b book the climbing wall for next weekend
c send Matt a message today

3

> **End of summer sale**
> **20% discount on all sandals and shorts!**

a The price of shorts and sandals has increased.
b You can buy some clothes at a lower price.
c You can buy all the clothes at a lower price.

4

> Students wanted, to help with park cleaning project on 7 October. We need at least twenty students, so bring a friend or family member if you want. If you're interested, sign your name below. It'll be messy work, so we suggest you wear some old clothes!

What do students who want to take part in the project have to do?

a sign the notice
b wear some old clothes
c bring other people

5

> Sarah
> Julia phoned and asked you to meet her at the shopping centre at 3 p.m. I've left you some money on the kitchen table – please get yourself some gloves.
> See you later
> Mum x

Sarah should

a phone Julia.
b ask her mum for some money.
c buy something.

6

> **Wanted**
> **Adventurous people who are not afraid of heights. Would you like to challenge yourself with a bungee jump? Sign up at letsbungee.com, but hurry – the first 100 people get a free place for them and a friend! Give it a go. You'll definitely get a buzz out of it!**

What do you need to do to get a free bungee jump?

a not be afraid of heights
b visit the website
c bring a friend

2 These people all want to try a new experience in the city where they live. Below there are descriptions of eight things to do. Decide which experience (A–H) would be the most suitable for each person (1–5).

Tip: Start by reading the descriptions of the people carefully. Next, read through the texts and underline any information which matches that in the descriptions. Finally, match the people with the texts.

1 ☐

Charlotte likes cooking and finds it relaxing, but is looking for a new challenge. She already knows how to make lots of different types of food, but would like to learn how to make different types of drinks.

2 ☐

Steve has lived in the same city all his life and always goes to the same places, so he's quite bored of it. He would like to travel and discover new places, but he doesn't have free time to do it.

3 ☐

Susan is interested in learning more about how to protect the environment. She feels disappointed when she sees how much rubbish there is on the streets of her city. She especially loves animals and loves learning all about them.

4 ☐

Joanna is really keen on fashion. She's been feeling bored with her appearance lately and would like to try something completely different. She doesn't really like big events and would like to spend some time experimenting with her appearance.

5 ☐

Higor feels annoyed when he sees how dirty the city is. He doesn't have many friends, but he would like to meet new people with similar interests. He's also interested in protecting the environment.

New experiences to try in the city

A Free fashion festival
This weekend, St. Helen's Park is filled with clothes, models and high fashion. Come along in the afternoon to see all the exciting, fashionable clothes we have to show. There will also be celebrity appearances from top designers and models, who will be signing copies of their books and speaking to members of the public.

B Become a barista!
Do you like nice coffee, but feel it's too expensive? Would you like to become king or queen of the coffee shop? Why not come along and learn how to make your own with this afternoon course? From sweet, spicy Mexican coffee to Indian coffee – learn how to make them all and impress your friends!

C Organise a local clean-up
Are you disappointed with all the litter in your area? Do you hate seeing rubbish in the street? Then get your friends together and organise a local clean-up group. You can also make new friends. We can send you bags and gloves, as well as information on how to recycle the things you find.

D Hidden city
If you're looking to have an adventure this summer, we offer tours to all those little places you never knew existed in the city. Hidden parks, specialist shops and quiet cafés are just a few of the places we'll help you to discover. We know where they all are – and so should you!

E Makeover time
Come and have a makeover! If you've been feeling worn-out and scruffy recently, then come and spend a few hours with us. Our stylists can give you advice on what clothes to wear. We can even paint your nails or dye your hair. So what are you waiting for? Come and give it a go.

F Rescue centre
Visit Tynedale Animal Shelter and find out about what we do. We have over 100 different species of endangered animals who we've rescued from captivity. Come and make friends with them today and discover how you can help protect them. This is a really fun day out and a truly enjoyable experience.

G Facing your fears
Are you afraid of heights? Visit our phobia centre, where we work with you to boost your confidence. We can also help with a fear of flying. At the end of the day with us, you get to climb our tower and we promise you'll get a buzz out of it!

H Cooking course
Does the thought of cooking make you feel stressed? If so, then our four-hour intensive cooking course is just for you. We show you how to make a range of delicious dishes from around the world and also give tips on what drinks go well with them. Challenge yourself to become a top chef!

3 Read the text and choose the correct letter (a, b, c or d) for each space.

Tip: Look at the example given at the beginning and think about *why* it's correct.

A brief history of teenage fashion

Although teenage fashion ¹___ existed before, it ²___ really become popular until the 1950s, when teenagers had more money. One of the earliest teenage fashions was the 'teddy boy'. Boys ³___ to wear long jackets, have short hair and long sideburns and wear big leather shoes. Polka-⁴___ skirts and dresses were popular with girls.

In the 1960s and 1970s teenagers became more important in society. They ⁵___ protesting against ⁶___-fashioned ways of doing things, which created the 'hippies'. These people wore baggy, flowery clothes and men grew their hair long. Later in the 1970s there was another protest movement – the 'punks'. This was an angry culture and punks liked to shock people. They wore ripped jeans and leather jackets, and ⁷___ lots of piercings. In the 1980s bright colours were fashionable. Lots of teenagers had dyed ⁸___ with lots of strange colours and wore big, bright jewellery.

These fashions may seem strange to look at now, but they had an important effect on society. Since the 1990s teenage fashion ⁹___ influenced all fashion. Teenagers ¹⁰___ starting the fashions which all age groups follow. Nowadays it isn't only teenagers who spend a lot of time trying to ¹¹___ good-looking!

	a		b		c		d
1	a was	b	hadn't	ⓒ	had	d	did
2	a wasn't	b	doesn't	c	weren't	d	didn't
3	a used	b	were	c	must	d	didn't
4	a stripe	b	dot	c	checked	d	striped
5	a had	b	were	c	was	d	did
6	a old	b	bad	c	used	d	plain
7	a have	b	wore	c	had	d	were
8	a freckles	b	hair	c	ears	d	complexion
9	a is	b	was	c	have	d	has
10	a are	b	were	c	is	d	was
11	a have	b	wear	c	do	d	be

4 For each question, complete the second sentence so that it means the same as the first. Use no more than three words.

Tip: When you've written your answer, read both sentences again carefully to make sure the meaning is exactly the same.

1 I bought this hoodie five years ago and I still have it now.
I _'ve had_ this hoodie for five years.

2 I put it on at noon and I'm still wearing it now.
I _____ it since noon.

3 I left the bottles at home, then I went to the bottle bank.
When I arrived at the bottle bank, I realised I _____ the bottles at home.

4 The radio was on at the same time as I got dressed.
While I was _____, the radio was on.

5 When I was younger, I didn't wear hoodies.
I didn't use _____ when I was younger.

6 I became ill on Monday. I'm still ill now.
I _____ since Monday.

5 Your friend Liz has invited you to be a model in a fashion show she is organising. Write an email to Liz. In your email, you should:
- accept the invitation.
- say what kind of clothes you like to wear.
- ask when it is.

Write **35–45 words**.

Tip: Make sure you include all three points.

6 Read the exam task. What do you have to do in your letter?

This is part of a letter you receive from an English friend.

Our class is planning a green project in the local community. Our teacher has asked us to think of ideas. What do you think we should do? Do you think we should ask people outside the class to help?

Now write a letter answering your friend's questions. Write your letter in about 100 words.

7 Match two of the verbs below with the groups of nouns 1–4.

clean up   damage   pollute   protect   ~~recycle~~   save   throw away   waste

1 _recycle_ / _____ plastic bags, aluminium cans, rubbish, litter, old clothes

2 _____ / _____ the air, rivers, canals, beaches, parks, lakes

3 _____ / _____ plants, animals, the environment, trees

4 _____ / _____ water, electricity, money, energy

8 Match 1–6 with a–f to make sentences.

1 [b] See   a with you?
2 [ ] What about   b you soon.
3 [ ] How are things   c save water is a good idea.
4 [ ] What have you been d make some posters?
5 [ ] Thinking of ways to e cleaning up the canal?
6 [ ] Why don't you   f up to?

9 Complete the categories with the sentences from Exercise 8.

Starting the letter
1 _____
Thanks for your letter.
2 _____
Sorry I haven't written sooner, but I've been busy.

Making suggestions
One thing you can try is writing to a politician.
Have you thought about starting a class blog?
3 _____
4 _____
You could/can save energy.
5 _____

Finishing a letter
Hope this helps.
Write back soon.
Bye (for now)/6 _____

10 Write your answer to the exam task in Exercise 6.

Tip: Plan your ideas before you write. Think of as many ideas as you can in two minutes, then choose the best two.

1 Look at the sentences about an online jobs fair. Read the text to decide if each sentence is correct (C) or incorrect (I).

Tip: Don't worry if there are words you don't know. Instead, focus on the specific information needed to decide if each statement is correct or incorrect.

1. ☐ This is the third jobs fair Emplotech has organised.
2. ☐ Emplotech helps firms find people to work for them.
3. ☐ You must register on 28 February.
4. ☐ Emplotech is the largest recruitment company in the world.
5. ☐ They look after people who are both working and unemployed.
6. ☐ The fair is at the weekend so that working people can take part.
7. ☐ Registering as a job candidate is a complicated process.
8. ☐ You send your CV directly to the company you want to work for.
9. ☐ You can have an interview online.
10. ☐ People who don't have a job pay half price to register.

Emplotech Online Jobs Fair

Emplotech will be offering its third annual online jobs fair on Saturday 15 March. We are the biggest recruitment company in the country and we have over twenty years' experience of organising jobs fairs and working in recruitment services. Our last two online jobs fairs were very successful, involving more than 200 big companies and 3,000 people looking for a job. Whether you are a company looking for the right person or someone looking for a (new) job, then our jobs fair is most definitely the place to be.

If you want to attend, you'll need to register by 28 February so that we have enough time to create your online 'space'. All you need to do is provide us with the information we need and we'll create an attractive page for you on our website.

We offer the following:

● For companies	● For candidates
We are the country's biggest provider of recruitment services. If you register with us, we'll give you access to thousands of people looking for a new job. We don't just work with unemployed people, but also highly skilled staff looking to change their careers. That's why the jobs fair is on a Saturday, not a working day. The people we work with are very ambitious and hard-working. Many companies have already benefitted from our experience in matching the right people with the right position. You can read reviews from satisfied customers on our website. Register your company for the online jobs fair online by visiting www.employtech.com/emp6.	We offer access to hundreds of companies looking for staff. If you want to find a new job, we will help you through the whole process. It's very easy and won't take you more than half an hour. First, write a CV and upload it to our website. Look at the jobs on offer and choose the ones that you want to apply for. If the company likes your CV, they will contact you and arrange a video interview using our website. If you're not successful, then at least you'll gain experience of applying and having an interview. This, at least, will give you a useful idea of the kinds of questions employers will ask you in an interview. What have you got to lose?

To register for the online jobs fair, please sign up at www.emplotech.com/ojf3. Registration costs £10. For people receiving unemployment benefit, registration costs £5.50. You must enter your National Insurance Number when registering.

2 Read the text and questions below. For each question (1–5), choose the correct letter (a, b, c or d).

Tip: Read the whole text quickly first. The first question is on the meaning and purpose of the text as a whole. Other questions ask about details, so you need to find the relevant parts which answer the questions. There are also questions about the writer's opinion and attitude.

My year in Sierra Leone
by Ann Chalmers

Two years ago I was working as a doctor at a hospital in London, when a colleague said to me, 'If you had the chance to change something in the world, what would you do?' At that time I told him that I hadn't thought about it before, so I didn't really know. But later that night I saw an advertisement in a magazine for Médecins Sans Frontières, a charity which sends doctors and medical staff to countries where there are emergency situations. I decided to call them and tell them that I wanted to help.

It took me six months to apply for the job because you have to do a lot of tests and paperwork. Finally, they told me I could go and they sent me to Sierra Leone. The healthcare system there was badly affected by the Ebola outbreak in 2014, but one of the biggest problems now is malaria. I worked in a small team of three and it was very hard work. If I'd known how hard it was, I would have prepared myself more carefully, I think. We worked very long hours, often into the night and although we had one day off per week, we often had to help out then too.

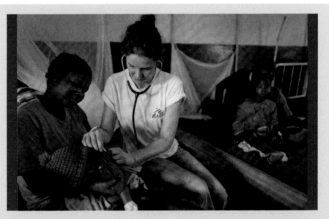

The hardest time was in the rainy season. The number of small children with malaria during this time almost doubled, but we didn't have any extra staff or facilities. If a child under five gets malaria, they need to see a doctor quickly or they might die. We also had to make a difficult decision sometimes: whether to send sick children to the hospital or keep them with us. It was a difficult journey to the hospital and if they were too ill, they wouldn't survive.

Although it was very difficult, I'm pleased I did it and I would do it again if I had the chance. It's difficult to see so many people so badly affected by diseases, but the small victories you have when you see people get better make it all worth it.

1 What is the writer trying to do in this text?
   a Advise people not to work with Médecins Sans Frontières.
   b Describe the good things and bad things about her year in Sierra Leone.
   c Show readers how good things are in Sierra Leone.
   d Say why you should work for Médecins Sans Frontières.

2 What made her decide to apply for Médecins Sans Frontières?
   a Médecins Sans Frontières called her.
   b Something she saw on TV.
   c Something she read.
   d A colleague told her she should do it.

3 What does she say about children under five who have malaria?
   a They need urgent medical attention.
   b They usually die.
   c They can't survive the journey to hospital.
   d She wanted to send them all to hospital.

4 What does she say about the experience at the end of the article?
   a She doesn't want to do it again.
   b She was afraid of getting ill.
   c It was very difficult to please the people she worked with.
   d It was hard, but she enjoyed it.

5 Which text message did she send home?
   a I'm having a great time at the weekends, seeing the country.
   b It's hard work here, but I only work four days a week.
   c The work here is difficult. The hours are long and I hate seeing so many people ill.
   d Things are very difficult here. There aren't many people ill, but it's difficult to watch them.

3 Look at the text in each question. What does it say? Choose the correct letter, a, b or c.

Tip: When you've chosen the answer, look back at the text to check that it is correct and that the meanings match.

1

Wanted
Part-time cook for temporary position over the summer. Weekday hours are flexible, but you must work on Saturdays. Ask inside for details.

a You only work at the weekend.
(b) You can choose your hours in the week.
c You only work on weekdays.

2

Our solar system was formed 4,568,000,000 years ago. The largest planets are Jupiter and Saturn, and these are made of gas. The smallest planet is Mercury, a very hot planet close to the sun.

a Our solar system is almost four billion years old.
b Jupiter and Saturn are the oldest planets in our solar system.
c Our solar system is over four billion years old.

3

This desk is for repeat prescriptions only, not for making appointments to see the doctor. Please tell us two days before you need your prescription and we will call you when it is ready for you to collect.

a You should request a repeat prescription at least two days in advance.
b It will take two days to write your prescription.
c You must make an appointment to see the doctor in order to get a prescription.

4

Phil,
Kevin called to say he can't make football practice tonight. His leg injury is better, but now he has the flu. The doctor told him to stay in bed and get some rest.
Mum

What's wrong with Kevin?
a He's ill.
b He has a leg injury.
c He has to see the doctor.

5

All students who want to take part in the work experience programme must bring a permission form signed by their parents by Thursday 13 March. Please hand your signed forms to Mr Davidson.

Students who want to do work experience should
a speak to Mr Davidson.
b complete a form.
c ask their parents to complete a form.

6

Mum,
I've got a temperature and I feel awful. I'm staying in bed at the moment. Can't find any medicine in the bathroom. Can you buy some on your way home?
Dan

Dan wants his mum to
a let him stay in bed.
b help him find the medicine.
c bring something to make him feel better.

4 For each question, complete the second sentence so that it means the same as the first. Use no more than three words.

Tip: Read the first sentence first. Then look at the second sentence and decide which words are the same and which are different from the first.

1 NASA have arranged to launch a spacecraft into space tomorrow.
NASA are _launching_ a spacecraft into space tomorrow.

2 The spacecraft is timetabled to leave at 7 a.m.
The spacecraft _____ at 7 a.m.

3 NASA said, 'We finished preparing the spacecraft yesterday.'
NASA said they _____ preparing the spacecraft the day before.

4 NASA said to the astronauts, 'Be ready to start at 5 a.m.'
NASA told the astronauts _____ at 5 a.m.

5 They wanted to launch the spacecraft last week, but the weather was bad.
If the weather hadn't been bad, they _____ the spacecraft last week.

6 They hope the weather is good so they can send the spacecraft into space.
If the weather is good, they _____ the spacecraft into space.

5 Your school is offering two-week work experience placements and has asked you to write and say what you would like to do. Write an email to your teacher. In your email, you should:
- say which job you would like to do.
- describe a useful skill you have for the job.
- ask when you'll find out about the job.

Write **35–45 words**.

Tip: Don't use a pre-prepared answer. This might not fit the topic in the exam and you won't get any marks.

6 Order phrases A–H to make a story. The first and last sentences are in the correct place.

A [1] It all began on Nick's first day at work as a lifeguard. It was a temporary job he was doing over the summer.

B [ ] When he reached her, he put his arm around her and pulled her back to the beach. The sea was strong and it was difficult to swim back.

C [ ] Later that day, he was having a great time relaxing by the beach, when all of a sudden he heard a scream out at sea.

D [ ] When he arrived, he introduced himself to his colleagues. After that, one of the other lifeguards showed him where to sit and watch the people in the sea.

E [ ] He was feeling sad on his way to work because he missed his girlfriend, Anna. She had broken up with him the day before.

F [ ] Finally, they got back to the beach and Nick saw who it was – Anna, his ex-girlfriend! He was so happy to see her.

G [ ] As if from nowhere, he saw a girl shouting and screaming in the sea. Nick jumped into the water and started swimming towards the girl.

H [8] They began talking and Anna explained that she had broken up with him because she had to move away to another city after the holidays and didn't want to hurt him. In the end, they decided to stay together for the summer and enjoy the time they had left.

7 Read the story again. Which sentences:
1 give the background of the story? [ ], [ ], [ ]
2 describe dramatic events? [ ], [ ], [ ]
3 give the final events/conclusion? [ ], [ ]

8 Complete the exam task below.

> Your English teacher has asked you to write a story. Your story must begin with the sentence:
>
> Fiona wanted to sit and cry. It had been a terrible day.
>
> Write your story in about 100 words.

Tip: Ask yourself questions (e.g. _Who? Why? How did they feel?_) to help you think of ideas for your story.

1 Read the text and choose the correct letter, a, b, c or d for each space.

Tip: Read the text quickly first, without looking at the answers. Try to predict what the missing word is before you look at the options.

PLATFORM ART

Banner Repeater is a cool little art gallery which ¹___ opened several years ago. It's an interesting idea for an art gallery and not in a location you'd usually expect to see one. It ²___ located on platform 1 of Hackney Downs train station in London. The gallery, ³___ you ⁴___ see exhibitions and performances by (inter)national and local artists, is named after a type of train signal. It gets its name from the function of the signal, which is basically just to repeat an earlier signal on the track, in case the driver ⁵___ able to see it the first time.

Art has ⁶___ exhibited ⁷___ (inter)national and local artists since it opened in 2010. It ⁸___ originally paid for by Art in Empty Spaces, Empty Shop Fund in its first year. Nowadays, it ⁹___ supported by various public funding institutions, as well as small donations by private benefactors. The artists ¹⁰___ exhibit in the gallery sometimes publish posters in the exhibition pamphlets, which you don't have ¹¹___ pay for, though you are welcome to make a donation if you want. If you are ever travelling through the station, leave home early so you have time to stop and enjoy the artwork.

1	ⓐ was	b	has	c	is	d	does
2	a will	b	has	c	is	d	was
3	a which	b	whose	c	when	d	where
4	a must	b	can	c	able	d	could
5	a wasn't	b	couldn't	c	didn't	d	could
6	a had	b	done	c	being	d	been
7	a to	b	for	c	by	d	with
8	a has	b	does	c	were	d	was
9	a is	b	has	c	was	d	are
10	a who's	b	whose	c	who	d	which
11	a the	b	must	c	a	d	to

2 These people all want to do something for a special occasion. Below are descriptions of eight things
to do. Decide which activity (A–H) would be the most suitable for each person (1–5).

Tip: Avoid just matching people to texts with the same words in. Make sure the information matches exactly.

1 ☐ Nathan is looking for somewhere to take his girlfriend for Valentine's Day. He'd like to take her somewhere romantic but today is 13 February, so he's left it quite late. She likes comedy, so it would be good if they could do something funny.

2 ☐ Harry is looking for somewhere to celebrate his birthday. He wants to have a good time with all his friends. He's into photography and loves taking photos and then sharing them on social networking sites.

3 ☐ Philippa is really into the arts and often reads books while she's eating when she's alone. She loves acting and knows the lines to many famous TV shows. She hopes to be a professional actor.

4 ☐ Fran is a very fussy eater – there are a lot of things she doesn't like to eat. She'd like to eat somewhere unusual, but doesn't have a lot of time because she has to catch a train later.

5 ☐ Anthony is looking for somewhere to go for a meal on his birthday with his parents. He would like to eat somewhere that is interesting visually. He's into technology and would love to try somewhere that makes use of this.

Special occasions

A Blind dining

Are you looking for a completely different eating experience? Come and try our tasting menu at The Night. At our restaurant, all dishes are served in the dark. You can't see a thing! We believe that by serving food in the dark, you are better able to taste all the different flavours. This will be a meal that you will remember for the rest of your life.

B Dinner with a view

If you're looking for a beautifully visual dinner experience, then why not come and have a meal at Night Tower? Our restaurant, which is on the fortieth floor, offers spectacular views of the city. It's always busy and fun, with a party atmosphere. The perfect place to celebrate a special occasion.

C Edible art

Here at Arty Edibles, not only is our food delicious, but all of our dishes are served as complete works of art. Each dish is designed by a local artist, then cooked by our top chefs. Each dish comes with a description by the artist. You can choose menus by theme, including abstract art, pop art, landscape dishes and even graffiti! Take a photo of your dish to share with friends, but don't forget to eat it!

D A literary experience

Step into a world of fiction as you eat, as all of our waiters are dressed as popular characters from films, plays and books. When they bring your food, they'll act a short scene from the story they appear in. We serve a wide range of dishes from Godfather-style Italian pasta to Willy Wonka's chocolate desserts. Each table has quotes from famous books and films. Guess where they're from and your drinks are free!

E Interactive dining

Come and visit Table Tech for a futuristic dining experience. Our interactive light projection system allows you to place your order with a 3D menu. And no more waiting to make eye contact with a waiter; simply select 'Service' on the table to call a waiter or waitress over. You can also choose from a range of virtual tablecloths and even order a taxi home, directly from your table.

F Personalised eating

Are you bored of menus which offer the same old dishes? Wish you could order *exactly* what you want in your meal? Here at Build-a-banquet, we offer you over 500 ingredients and you create your own dish. Each table has a tablet you can use to make your choices and calculate the cost too. Once you've decided, simply hit 'Send' and your meal will be with you in twenty minutes.

G A romantic evening

If you want to make your loved one feel special, there's no better place than À la Parisienne. Our authentic French dishes are served by candlelight in a charming atmosphere. While you wait for your meal, our in-house musicians will come to your table and sing soft, romantic songs to serenade you (you can make requests for songs beforehand). It's the perfect place to celebrate Valentine's Day, but book early as our tables are limited.

H Pop Café

Our restaurant is the perfect place for music lovers. All of our waiters are trained musicians and each dish is served with a pop song, adapted to the dish you order. From *Can't Stop the Eating* to *Cheese Thrills* to *Don't Let Me Bread*, you'll love our food-based versions of pop songs. Just remember: don't sing with your mouth full!

3 Look at the sentences about a visit to a festival. Read the text to decide if each sentence is correct (C) or incorrect (I).

Tip: The sentences are in the same order as the answers in the text. First, read the sentences, then scan the text to find the answer to the first sentence. Repeat this for the rest of the sentences.

1 ☐ The carnival started in the seventeenth century.

2 ☐ Over two million people take part in each parade.

3 ☐ The writer saw more than two famous places on the journey from the airport.

4 ☐ The parades take place on only two nights, but carnival is longer.

5 ☐ The samba school parades are in a football stadium.

6 ☐ The competition is very important for Brazilians.

7 ☐ The writer's costume looked like a humming bird.

8 ☐ The writer danced in the parade for two nights.

9 ☐ The music was louder than the spectators.

10 ☐ Beija-flor didn't win the competition.

My carnival experience

I'm a member of a dance group and earlier this year I won a prize to go to Rio de Janeiro in Brazil and take part in what many people believe is the largest festival on Earth – the Rio carnival. The carnival has been running since 1723 and it gets bigger each year. This year there were over two million people on the streets, dancing and singing in street parties, or 'balls'.

I arrived a few days before, after a twelve-hour overnight flight from London, so I was very tired. The director of the samba school met me and drove me to the fashionable district of Ipanema, where I was staying in a hostel. On the way, we passed lots of impressive sights, including Sugarloaf Mountain and the famous Copacabana beach, which was awesome.

Carnival officially starts on Friday and goes on all the next week, but the atmosphere in the city is very exciting for days before that. I was taking part in the parade with the samba school Beija-Flor (Humming Bird), one of the most famous schools in Rio. On Saturday and Sunday nights, the samba schools parade in the Sambadrome, a special stadium in the centre of the city. The stadium is only used for carnival and a group of judges choose the best parade. The competition is very important and Brazilians take it very seriously, so I had to learn how to do the dance, including all the correct facial expressions and gestures.

When I arrived at the samba school, the first thing they did was fit my costume. The theme of the parade this year was the history of Brazil and the costume was designed to look like the Sabiá-laranjeira, a bird which is one of the national symbols of Brazil. For the next two days I practised the dance with the rest of the samba school. It was hard work, especially because the temperature was over thirty-five degrees!

Finally, on Saturday night it was time for our parade. We arrived at the Sambadrome at midnight, but we weren't on until 3 a.m. None of us were tired though, because we were all so nervous! The place was amazing. There were thousands of spectators and you could hear them cheer and clap above the noise of the drums and singing. As we walked out, dancing and singing, I felt happier than I'd ever felt before in my life. At the end of our parade, we had a fireworks display with the colours of the Brazilian flag. I was tired and my legs hurt, but it was worth it. The next day I slept all day!

On Wednesday the winner was announced. It wasn't our samba school – we came third. I was really happy with that. Altogether, it was an unforgettable experience. If you ever have the chance to take part in the Rio carnival, then say 'Yes'!

4 For each question, complete the second sentence so that it means the same as the first. Use no more than three words.

Tip: Once you have written your answer, read both sentences again. Make sure both sentences have exactly the same meaning and that you've spelt the words in the second sentence correctly.

1 How old are you?
  Could you tell me how _old you are_?

2 Jude Harcliff wrote *Every Summer Night*.
  Every Summer Night
  _____ Jude Harcliff.

3 She tried to write it in one month and she succeeded.
  She _____ write it in one month.

4 It was necessary for her to go and live alone in the mountains to write it.
  She had _____
  and live alone in the mountains to write it.

5 That's a hotel. Robert de Niro stayed there when he was filming *Heist*.
  That's the hotel
  _____ Robert de Niro stayed while he was filming *Heist*.

6 Did she enjoy the experience?
  Do you know _____
  the experience?

5 Your friend Jill has invited you to her leaving party, but you can't go. Write a note to Jill. In your note, you should:

- apologise to Jill.
- Say why you can't go.
- suggest another time you can meet her.

Write **35–45 words**.

Tip: Don't forget to address your message to the person named in the task and don't forget to write your name at the end.

6 Read the exam task. Then look at ideas a–h below, which will help you plan your message. Tick the five ideas which are relevant to the topic of the letter.

> This is part of a letter you receive from an English friend.
>
> We had a great time this New Year's Eve. What's your favourite celebration and why do you like it? What are you going to do for your next birthday?
>
> Now write a letter answering your friend's questions. Write your letter in about 100 words.

a ✓ the reason for/background to the favourite celebration
b ☐ a celebration you don't enjoy
c ☐ things you do and eat/drink during the celebration
d ☐ your favourite thing about the celebration
e ☐ what you did for your last birthday
f ☐ a description of where you live
g ☐ where you will celebrate your birthday
h ☐ who you will celebrate your birthday with

7 Read the exam task. Choose the correct option to complete the phrases which will be useful in the story.

> Your teacher has asked you to write a story.
> This is the title of your story:
>
> A case of bad communication
>
> Write your story in about 100 words.

1 It all started *which / when* Chris shook his head.
2 At *that / the* moment, I knew he was lying.
3 The *second / seconds* I looked him in the eye, he looked away.
4 Out of the *green / blue*, I received a text message.
5 Later *the / that* day, the phone was disconnected.
6 After *that / then*, I walked up to her and gave her a hug.
7 When it was all *under / over*, I realised I'd made a huge mistake.
8 *Final / Finally*, we realised it had all just been a misunderstanding.

8 Write your answer to one of the exam tasks in Exercises 6 and 7.

Unit 1

Exercise 1
1 surprised 2 uneasy 3 take 4 punctual
5 generous 6 boost

Exercise 2
1 be 2 surprise 3 tell 4 express
5 Know 6 congratulate

Exercise 3
1 are staying 2 gets up 3 is 4 am having
5 isn't enjoying 6 Does your mum like

Exercise 4
1 were having 2 didn't pass 3 has never
climbed 4 wasn't 5 went 6 was watching

Exercise 5
1 have always loved 2 decided 3 was
4 saw 5 talked 6 were walking 7 were
waiting 8 met 9 invited

Exercise 6
1 mind, not 2 get, fine 3 hand, nice
4 help, minute 5 give, can

Unit 2

Exercise 1
1 factory 2 smoke 3 pollute 4 damaged
5 petrol station

Exercise 2
1 throw away 2 endangered animals
3 climate change 4 public transport
5 renewable energy

Exercise 3
1 had got up 2 had organised
3 had signed up 4 had been 5 had done
6 had dropped 7 had collected

Exercise 4
1 used to play 2 didn't use to live 3 used to
recycle 4 Did Hannah use to go, did 5 didn't
use to have 6 Did Luke use to be, didn't

Exercise 5
1 You don't like tea, do you? 2 Plastic bags
pollute the ocean, don't they? 3 They didn't use
to recycle, did they? 4 We forgot to switch off
the lights, didn't we? 5 Climate change is a big
problem, isn't it? 6 The government won't do
enough, will they?

Exercise 6
1 totally 2 say 3 agree 4 so 5 sure

Unit 3

Exercise 1
1 gloves 2 scruffy 3 wellies 4 button
5 pale 6 tracksuit

Exercise 2
1 c 2 e 3 a 4 d 5 b 6 f

Exercise 3
1 have been working, since 2 has been
studying, since 3 has been running, all
4 haven't been waiting, for 5 have been
making, for 6 hasn't been writing, since

Exercise 4
1 have you known 2 has had 3 have you been
wearing 4 I've eaten 5 have been waiting

Exercise 5
1 have been tidying 2 have found
3 have had 4 have grown
5 have been thinking 6 have found
7 have been doing 8 haven't finished

Exercise 6
1 nice/great, think 2 really, nice 3 were,
made 4 got, day 5 nice/lovely, so

Unit 4

Exercise 1
1 scientist 2 cleaner 3 travel agent 4 cook
5 fashion designer 6 writer

Exercise 2
1 unemployment benefit 2 wage 3 shift
4 bonus 5 temporary job 6 pension

Exercise 3
1 am going to watch 2 will make
3 will pass 4 leaves 5 am going

Exercise 4
1 will be living 2 will be moving 3 will
be working 4 won't be doing 5 will be
studying 6 will be applying

Exercise 5
1 about 2 on 3 of 4 in 5 for 6 with

Exercise 6
1 few 2 important 3 sure, That 4 to, No
5 Then, that

Unit 5

Exercise 1
1 engine 2 satellite 3 galaxy 4 orbit
5 atmosphere 6 Gravity

Exercise 2
1 million 2 astronomer 3 comet
4 solar system 5 width 6 telescope
7 height 8 planet

Exercise 3
1 had, 2 2 go, 0 3 have met, 3
4 won't come, 1 5 were, 2 6 wins, 1
7 had left, 3 8 travel, 0

Exercise 4
1 will achieve 2 study 3 won
4 would buy 5 don't/won't have
6 play 7 go 8 would you do

Exercise 5
1 had remembered, wouldn't have laughed
2 would have stayed, hadn't been 3 wouldn't
have been, had worn 4 would have been, hadn't
fallen 5 had turned off, wouldn't have rung

Exercise 6
1 allowed 2 Watch 3 out 4 Make
5 off 6 careful

Unit 6

Exercise 1
1 hay fever 2 injury 3 travel sickness
4 allergy 5 bug 6 abseiling

Exercise 2
1 operation 2 asthmatic 3 stressed
4 painful 5 sickness

Exercise 3
1 had 2 was 3 was 4 that 5 would
6 wanted 7 didn't 8 would 9 him
10 didn't

Exercise 4
1 The doctor told me to stay in bed.
2 I asked my friend to help me change my
bandage. 3 The nurse told him to take that
medicine twice a day. 4 Sally asked us to be
quiet. 5 Kevin's mum told him not to touch that.

Exercise 5
1 Both 2 nor 3 none 4 any 5 either

Exercise 6
1 Any, you 2 advice, something, good
3 would, going, know

Unit 7

Exercise 1
1 billboard 2 body contact 3 expressions
4 flyer 5 commercials 6 voice

Exercise 2
1 interrupt 2 definition 3 repeat 4 describe/
described 5 discussion 6 suggestion
7 communication 8 explain

Exercise 3
1 c 2 b 3 e 4 a 5 f 6 d

Exercise 4
1 were given lots of homework by our Maths
teacher 2 is played in Brazil 3 has been
advertised on billboards 4 must be followed at
all times 5 can't be taken in here 6 has been
announced by Flyby

Exercise 5
1 will be opened 2 will be offered
3 will be taught 4 will be included
5 will be built 6 will be located

Exercise 6
1 mean 2 here 3 the 4 that 5 it 6 could
7 When 8 say 9 that/which 10 them

Unit 8

Exercise 1
1 graffiti 2 portrait 3 broadsheet 4 sketch
5 designer 6 weather forecast 7 headlines
8 plot

Exercise 2
1 novelist 2 biography 3 play 4 author
5 novel 6 playwright

Exercise 3
1 wasn't able to visit 2 Will you be able to return
3 couldn't swim 4 Did you manage to finish
5 won't be able to go 6 can't speak

Exercise 4
1 do we have to, have to 2 Were, had
3 to leave, won't 4 Is, is allowed to 5 must,
don't have to

Exercise 5
1 in 2 in 3 on 4 at 5 on 6 by 7 on
8 on 9 in 10 at

Exercise 6
1 On 2 the 3 In 4 seems 5 see 6 totally/
completely 7 concerned 8 ask

Unit 9

Exercise 1
1 prom 2 ceremony 3 festival
4 get-together 5 house-warming
6 New Year's Eve party 7 dinner
8 Mother's Day

Exercise 2
Across
1 decorations 4 symbol 7 fireworks 8 hired
Down
2 celebrate 3 street 5 costume 6 toast

Exercise 3
1 whose, D 2 which, ND 3 who, ND
4 where, D 5 where, ND 6 whose, D

Exercise 4
1 Could you tell me what time the parade
starts? 2 I was wondering where the nearest
station is. 3 Do you know if Mark is coming
to the party? 4 Can you tell me how old you
are? 5 Do you know if the tickets are expensive?

Exercise 5
1 got 2 to 3 could 4 plans 5 visit
6 going 7 to